Credit
+
Budget
=
Control

Improve Your Life Immediately!

Jeni Temen

©2020 by Jeni Temen
Credit+Budget=Control
Improve Your Life Immediately!

All rights reserved. No part of this book may be reproduced in whole or part, or stored in a retrieval system, or transmitted in any form or by any means, electronic, mechanical, photocopying, recording, or otherwise, without the written permission of the author.
ISBN: 978-1-7345015-4-4
Library of Congress Control Number: 2020922412
Printed in Cedarville, California, USA by R Money Club

The publisher has strived to be as accurate and complete as possible in the creation of this book. This book is not intended for use as a source of legal, health, medical, business, accounting, or financial advice. All readers are advised to seek the services of competent professionals in legal, health, medical, business, accounting, and financial fields.

The advice and strategies found within may not be suitable for every situation. This work is sold with the understanding that neither the author nor the publisher is held responsible for the results accrued from the advice in this book. While all attempts have been made to verify information provided for this publication, the publisher assumes no responsibility for errors, omissions, or contrary interpretation of the subject matter herein. Because of the dynamic nature of the Internet, any web addresses or links contained in this book may have changed since publication of this book and may no longer be valid.

"All successful people, men and women, are big dreamers. They imagine what their future could be, ideal in every respect, and then they work every day toward their distant vision, that goal or purpose"

- Brian Tracy

Your Credit Matters

Table of Contents

Introduction	. 09
1.) First Things First – Your Credit Report.	. 13
2.) FICO and You	. 33
3.) Next Things Next – Finding Your Score	. 37
4.) Establishing Good Credit.	. 41
5.) Repairing Your Credit Score	. 47
6.) Bankruptcy.	. 55
Chapter 7	. 57
Chapter 11.	. 61
Chapter 13	. 65
7.) Credit Counselors/Debt Consolidators	. 71
8.) Mistakes can be made.	. 81
9.) Identity Theft and Your Credit.	.89
10.) Raising Your Credit Score.	.99
11.) To Review.	.103
12.) Conclusion	.111

Your Family Budget

Table of Contents

1.) Family Budgets: A brief introduction . 117
2.) Why a book on setting up a family budget? . 125
3.) Do you need a family budget?.`. . . 127
4.) Benefits and advantages of a family budget 135
5.) The rationale and process of budgeting . . 139
6.) Top three causes of budget failure. . . 143
7.) Family budgets defined. . . . 147
8.) How to set up a good family budget . . 151
9.) Hints, tips, tolls and tricks for setting up a family budget 163
10) Here are eleven practical suggestions and tips 174
11) How should a family budget be used . 187
12.) Final thoughts on setting up a family budget 201
14.) Tips and ideas for teaching kids about money 205
15.) Money saving ideas 209

Your Credit Matters

Introduction

We are a country in debt. Not only is our government in debt, but we, as Americans, are in debt ourselves, and the problem is just getting worse! Recent studies have shown that ninety percent of Americans have at least one credit card – and they are using that card – A Lot!

The average family carries a balance of between $7,000 and $10,000 on all their credit cards. Over $1,000 per family goes on interest every year. And that's just the average – some people owe much more!

Overall, Americans spend over $1 trillion every year on their credit cards and owe more than $500 billion of it. If debt continues at the current rate, then one family in a hundred will be forced into bankruptcy. Over 90% of Americans' disposable incomes are spent paying back debts.

When you add credit card debt to the regular bills, we have to pay each month, which can tax anyone's budget. As a result, some bills go unpaid and others are paid late.

Both of these instances can damage your credit sometimes so much that you think there's no way you'll ever be able to get out of debt and get credit for something important like a home or a car.

The truth is that you can get out of debt and repair your credit nearly to what it was before you had credit problems. It takes some time and a little work on your part, but it IS possible.

Loan approvals and such depend on your credit score. That number is what determines if you can get credit, what your interest rate will be, and how much money potential lenders will give you. A good median score is 720, but the higher your score is, the more financially sound you are.

While it's always a good idea to try and stay away from credit, not everyone has a hundred thousand dollars lying around to buy a home or twenty thousand to buy a car. Heck, for some people, scraping together five thousand dollars for a good used car is difficult. That's why we need credit. So, we can buy that which we cannot afford.

Where the trouble comes in is when people begin to buy everyday items such as groceries and clothing on credit cards. Then those bills begin to get bigger and bigger until pretty soon, they're paying the minimum amount due which will take forever to pay off. Plus, a lot of people just continue charging things even when they have a large balance on their account.

Your credit score defines who you are to businesses and you want it to be as high as it can be. It doesn't matter how bad your credit is now. There are ways that you can raise your credit score no matter how low it is now. Don't despair; just get started – right away!

Jeni Temen

First Things First
Your Credit Report

The very first step you need to take when trying to raise your credit score is to find out what your score is and what it means. Legislation called the **FACT ACT** was passed that allows all Americans to get one free copy of their credit report every year. This report lists all of your debts you've had and your payment history on those debts.

It will tell you where you owe money, how much you owe, and how you pay (on time, 30 days late, etc.). All of that information is compiled together and then analyzed.

After the analysis, a number is assigned to you as to what your credit fitness level is. Potential creditors then look at your credit score and decide if you are going to be able to pay back the amount of money you are requesting to borrow.

That's the short version. Actually, there is much, much more involved in determining your credit score. However, what should be important to you is knowing how to read your credit report and how to raise that score so that you are able to get the things you need. Remember that – the things you **NEED**, not the things you **WANT**!

Let's start with how to get your credit report in the first place. There are three major credit reporting agencies that will offer you the one free credit report you get each year. They are Experian, TransUnion, and Equifax. You can contact each of them directly in the following ways:

Equifax
Online, you can find them at www.equifax.com
You can also order your free credit report by mail. However, they only offer this option for free to residents in the states of Colorado, Georgia, Maine, Maryland, Massachusetts, New Jersey, and Vermont. All other states are required to pay a $10 fee.

If you do want to do this by mail, send your request to:
Equifax Information Services, LLC
Disclosure Department
P.O. Box 740241; Atlanta, GA 30374.
You can also call them at 1-800-685-1111.

TransUnion
Their web address is www.transunion.com
As with Equifax, you can also make your request via mail by getting a copy of their mail request form

online and sending it to the address provided. You can also call them at 1-877-322-8228.

Experian

Their web address is www.experian.com
As with TransUnion, you will need to download a form from their website if you wish to request your credit report by mail. By phone you can call 888 397 3742.

Here are other websites who will also allow you to download your free credit report:

- www.annualcreditreport.com
- www.freecreditreport.com
- www.creditreport.com
- www.freecreditreportinstantly.com

The main thing is that you will want to get your free credit report in order to find out where you stand and how far you have to go to repair your credit. Most of the time when you download your credit report, you will be able to view and save it instantly. Save it to your computer's "My Documents" file if you can. That way you'll be able to print it out and refer to it as much as you need.

Also, some of these sites offer low-cost memberships that will alert you if a new item comes onto your credit report. Their services will offer many different things, but purchasing a membership is strictly voluntary and probably not necessary if you want the straight truth.

Once you get a copy of your credit report, it's important to know how to read it. There are going to be an awful lot of numbers, abbreviations and terms you've never seen before. Trade lines, charge-offs, account review inquiries -- how do you read this thing?

Even though you get one free credit report each year, experts suggest that if you are serious about improving your credit score, you need to examine a report from each of the three major credit reporting agencies. This will, however cost you a small fee from the other two, so keep that in mind.

Why do they suggest you have all three?

Creditors can pick and choose which credit reporting agency they want to report to. Some will report to all three, but many won't. You may find that what is included on one report isn't on another. The reports will have different information because it's a voluntary system, and creditors subscribe to whichever agency they want -- if any at all.

A credit report is basically divided into four sections: identifying information, credit history, public records and inquiries.

Identifying information is just that -- information to identify you. Look at it closely to make sure it's accurate. It's not unusual for there to be two or three spellings of your name or more than one Social Security number. That's usually because someone reported the information that way. The variations will stay on your credit report. If it's reported wrong, leave it because it might mess up the link. Don't be concerned about variations.

Other information in this section might include your current and previous addresses, your date of birth, telephone numbers, driver's license numbers, your employer and your spouse's name. The data in this section is often used to verify your identity or to confirm that the information you provided for an application is accurate. Small variations in this data between the three bureaus are normal as each agency may have their own recording procedures.

The personal information section of your credit report may also include a "consumer statement." This is a statement that you asked the credit reporting agencies to add to your report. Commonly, this statement is used to explain a record on your report.

For example, "The Smith Bank account from 2004 was a shared account with my ex-husband." This statement does not impact your credit score but may help you clarify a situation to a potential creditor or lender and improve your chances to obtain credit.

The next section in your credit history. Sometimes, the individual accounts are called trade lines. Each account will include the name of the creditor and the account number, which may be scrambled for security purposes.

You may have more than one account from a creditor. Many creditors have more than one kind of account, or if you move, they transfer your account to a new location and assign a new number.

The entry will also include:

- When you opened the account

- The kind of credit (installment, such as a mortgage or car loan, or revolving, such as a department store credit card)

- Whether the account is in your name alone or with another person

- Total amount of the loan, high credit limit or highest balance on the card

- How much you still owe minimum monthly amount

- Fixed monthly payments or interest and principal

- Status the account (open, inactive, closed, paid, etc.)

- How well you've paid the account

On Experian's report, your payment history is written in plain English -- never pays late, typically pays 30 days late, etc. Other comments might include internal collection and charged off or default. Charged off means the creditor has given up, thrown in the towel. Basically, the company has made efforts to collect the debt, realized that it's not going to be paid, and subsequently wrote it off.

Other reports use payment codes ranging from 1 to 9; an R1 or I1 on a report is an indication of a good payment history on a revolving or installment account. Often, the code key will be listed on the report so you can better understand what the codes mean, but they may not.

Credit accounts are divided into five categories: real estate, installment, revolving, collection and other. Here is a better description of each category:

- Real Estate:

First and second mortgage loans on your home.

- Installment:

Accounts comprised of fixed terms with regular payments, such as a car loan.

- Revolving:

Accounts with opened terms with varying payments, such as a credit card account.

- Collection:

Accounts seriously past due that have been assigned to an attorney or collection agency.

- Other:

Accounts where the exact category is unknown. This could include 30-day accounts, such as an American Express card.

Your credit report lists a summary of the details and terms for each account. This summary includes information about the account number, condition, balance, type and pay status for each account. The summary for collection records is slightly different.

The following information is for real estate, installment, revolving and other type records:

- Creditor:

The official account names. This name may be different than you expect if your account is managed by a larger financial corporation.

- Account Number:

This is an identifying number for your account. Typically, this would be a credit card number for a credit card account or a loan identification number for a mortgage. A portion of the number is hidden for security reasons. A partial account number is all that is needed to file a dispute about the record.

- Condition:

This is the account's status as open or closed, according to the most recent update from your creditor.

- Balance:

The amount you presently owe on the account based on the last reported activity. Very recent activities may not yet have appeared in the bureaus' computer system so this balance may be a few days out-of-date.

- Type:

The account's specific type. Some common types are real estate, automobile, educational and credit card accounts.

- Pay Status:

The account's payment status, according to the most recent update from your creditor.

For each account, the report also displays an illustrated payment history over the last 24 months. There will be a key at the top of this section describes each payment history symbol and what it indicates for your account. Green boxes marked "OK" show that your payment was made on time.

Most credit reports also give you more in-depth information about specific accounts. This is also an important part of the credit report you'll want to review for accuracy.

The following information may be reported for your account in this section:

- Past Due:

The amount of payment overdue as of the most recent reported activity. Very recent payments may take a few days to appear on your credit report.

- High Balance:

The most you have ever owed on this account. In the case of a credit card, this is the highest balance you've ever charged. For a mortgage, it is the initial amount of the mortgage.

- Terms:

This is the number of payments you have scheduled with a creditor. Most commonly this applies to loan accounts. For example, an auto loan may have a repayment plan scheduled over 36 months and a home loan may have a repayment plan scheduled over 360 months.

- Opened:

The date the account was opened.

- Limits: For a credit card or other revolving account, this is the maximum amount you are approved to borrow.

- Payment:

This is the minimum amount you are required to pay each month toward the account.

- Reported:

The last date when any activity for this account was shown. Activities include payments, credit card billings and changes in your terms. Very recent activity may not yet show on your account, since it takes time for it to appear in the credit reporting agency's system.

- Responsibility:

This indicates your responsibility for the account. For example individual, joint or co-signer.

- Late Payments:

A summary of your 30, 60- and 90-day late payments over the past 7 years. Please note that the figures in the seven-year history include any late payments shown in the two-year history.

- Remarks:

Notes about the status or condition of your account.

Collection accounts are accounts that are seriously past due and have been transferred to an attorney, collection agency or creditor's internal collection agency. As your debt is transferred between different agencies, you may see several records on your report for the same debt. Only one record should be marked as open at a time. All the collection records and the original debt record will expire from your credit report at the same time. Collection records use a unique summary format on your credit report:

- Creditor Name: The official name of the company that is currently attempting to collect the debt.

- Account Number:

An identifying number for your account with the collection agency. This is not the same as the account number on your original debt.

- Original Creditor:

The name of the original creditor where you accumulated your debt. This could be an account that is listed on your credit report (such as a credit card) or an account that is not listed on your report (such as a library, video rental or cell phone company). If this creditor was a medical office, the name may be masked for your privacy.

- Responsibility:

This indicates your responsibility for the account.

For example, individual, joint or co-signer.

- Condition:

The current status of your collection record. For example, open, closed or paid.

- Original Balance:

The amount of debt owed on the original account before it was transferred.

- Date Opened:

The date the account was transferred to the collection agency.

- Date Reported:

The date of the collection agency's last update to this account record.

- Remarks:

Notes about the account as reported to each credit reporting agency. For example, this section may note that the collector has been unable to locate you or that you have not yet paid the debt.

The next section is the part you want to see absolutely blank. The public records section is never a good story. If you have a public record on there, you've had a problem that has required litigation. It doesn't list arrests and criminal activities ;just financial-related data, such as bankruptcies, judgments and tax liens. Those are the monsters that will trash your credit faster than anything else.

Here are definitions of the eight types of public records you could see listed on your credit report:

- Bankruptcy:

A legal filing that relieves a person of responsibility for all or some of their debts because they are unable to pay.

- Tax Lien:

A claim filed by a local, state or federal tax agency against a person who owes back taxes.

- Legal Item:

A general filing. This is most commonly a judgment against you in civil action.

- Marital Item:

A legal filing related to a marital or divorce issue.

- Financial Counseling:

A public record indicating that a person has participated in financial counseling.

- Financial Statement:

A type of lien filed by a creditor against a person's property. This can be filed when a loan is secured against personal property.

- Foreclosure:

A record indicating that a mortgaged property has been taken over by the creditor because the borrower has defaulted on the loan.

- Garnishment:

A record indicating a court order to withhold some or all of a person's wages to repay a debt owed to a creditor.

The summary information listed for each of these types of public records can vary. Here are some definitions of common record categories:

- Type: The type of record. For example, a tax lien, bankruptcy, garnishment, or judgment.
- Status:

Current status of the record. For example, released, filed or dismissed.

- Date Filed/Reported:

Date when the record was initially filed or created.

- How Filed:

The role that you played in the public record. Usually the record is filed either individually or jointly.

- Reference Number:

Identifying number for the record.

- Released/Closing Date:

Date when the record was closed, released or judgment was awarded.

- Court:

The court or legal agency that has jurisdiction over the record.

- Plaintiff:

The plaintiff in the case of a legal judgment.

- Amount:

Dollar amount of the lien or judgment.

- Remarks:

Notes regarding the public record as reported to the credit bureaus. If the public record is a bankruptcy, three other fields will be visible.

- Liability:

The amount the court found you to be legally responsible to repay.

- Exempt Amount:

The dollar amount claimed against you that the court has decided you are not legally responsible for.

- Asset Amount:

The dollar amount of total personal assets used in the court's decision. The Asset Amount can include items of value that can be used to pay debts.

The final section is the inquiries. That's a list of everyone who asked to see your credit report. Any time anyone gets into the report, it'll post an inquiry.

That means if you try to apply for a credit card, it's listed as an inquiry. Have you been shopping for a car? Every time a dealership runs a credit report, it shows. If you call the credit bureau and ask for a copy, it will be on there. It's a very detailed entry record. Generally, this is great for the consumer.

Inquiries are divided into two sections.

"Hard" inquiries are ones you initiate by filling out a credit application or taking your child to the orthodontist.

"Soft" inquiries are from companies that want to send out promotional information to a pre-qualified group or current creditors who are monitoring your account.

You may have heard that a large number of inquiries can have a negative impact on your credit score, but you're probably OK. The vast majority of inquiries are ignored by the FICO scoring models. They're not the steak in the steak dinner, so to speak.

For instance, the model has a buffer period that ignores inquiries within 30 days of getting a mortgage or a car loan. It also counts two or more "hard" inquiries in the same 14-day period as just one inquiry. You could have 30 in two weeks and it only counts as one.

However, on the other hand, having a lot of credit inquiries on your account could also show potential creditors that you are trying to live your life on credit which means you might not have the means to pay back the debt. This is especially true if you've been applying for a lot of credit cards. And there are always many opportunities to apply for a credit card.

Of course, you know about all of the offers that come in the mail. They usually read "You've Been Approved!" as an enticement for filling out the application. This is not always true with pre-approval offers, so proceed carefully. I usually shred them up and forget them.

Another time that you will be asked to apply for credit occurs in public places and the companies are offering products for free in exchange for a credit application. I was at a baseball game recently and one credit card company was offering free team T-shirts and all I had to do was fill out their credit card application. I didn't do it, but what an enticement – especially for a fan!

Watch out, too, when you are shopping at your favorite department stores. They also have store credit cards and may offer you a percentage off your purchase in exchange for a credit application. In general, this is not a bad idea – which we will talk about a little later in rebuilding your credit – because store credit cards are great when helping to rebuild your credit.

The bottom line is that if you don't need another credit card, don't apply for one. It's always good to have one on hand for emergencies, but having five or six can just be a temptation to spend beyond your means.

There may also be a section on your credit report that lists creditor information. The creditor contact section lists the name and contact information for each creditor that appears on your credit report. This can also include the contact
information for creditors that have made inquiries.

Each creditor's address is listed to the right of the creditor's name. When available, a phone number is listed for the creditor. Creditors without listed numbers should be contacted by mail.

So that's the first step – getting your credit report and going over it with a fine tooth comb. But where's that magic number – your credit score? Let's begin with a short section on the credit score itself and where it comes from.

FICO and You

"All successful people, men and women, are big dreamers. They imagine what their future could be, ideal in every respect, and then they work every day toward their distant vision, that goal or purpose"
-Brian Tracy

Back in the 1960's, a company called Fair Isaac devised a unique system to determine the credit worthiness of people who apply for loans. Through a complicated mathematical computation (too complicated for this author!), they were able to study a person's credit history and assign them a number that would represent how likely it was that they would be able to repay a loan they were applying for.

Fair Isaac sparked a revolution by pioneering credit risk scoring for the financial services industry. This new approach to lending enabled financial institutions to improve their business performance and expand consumers' access
to credit. Today Fair Isaac's FICO score is widely recognized as the industry standard for lenders.

The FICO score condenses a borrower's credit history into a single number based on past credit history.

Fair, Isaac & Co. and the credit bureaus do not reveal how these scores are computed. The Federal Trade Commission has ruled this to be acceptable. The real truth is that even if we did know, we probably couldn't calculate it ourselves anyway. Unless, of course, you happen to be a mathematical genius!

Credit scores are calculated by using scoring models and mathematical tables that assign points for different pieces of information which best predict future credit performance. Developing these models involves studying how thousands, even millions, of people have used credit.

Score-model developers find predictive factors in the data that have proven to indicate future credit performance. Models can be developed from different sources of data. Credit-bureau models are developed from information in consumer credit-bureau reports.

Credit scores analyze a borrower's credit history considering numerous factors such as:

There are really three FICO scores computed by data provided by each of the three bureaus—Experian, Trans Union and Equifax. Some lenders use one of these three scores, while other lenders may just use the middle score.

Fair Isaac has become so important in the financial industry that their word on your credit has become basically the final word. Why would banks and creditors place so much credibility into one company? The answer is simply because of their proven track record.

The FICO score has proven to be not only an accurate and amazingly consistent way of showing a person's credit reliability, but it has also saved companies millions of dollars in credit write-offs due to bad lending decisions. A study of loans that were granted and/or denied simply due to the FICO scores shows that Fair Isaac has been right over 80 percent of the time.

Of course, that required some chance taking on the part of many creditors, but they were willing to take the risk. After all, this was a ground-breaking thing determining credit worthiness through a simple three-digit number. Many companies jumped "on the bandwagon" just to show that Fair Isaac had the right idea.

Fast forward to the twenty-first century and you will find that FICO has become the definitive when it comes to financial and credit matters. They have proven their reliability and their worthiness just through trial and error.

Unfortunately, the problem is that finding your FICO score isn't as easy as you think. The truth is that it's not even shown on your credit report like you would think. In fact, for years and years, your credit score was a securely kept secret number that was elusive to the average person.

Next Things Next - Finding Your Score

You would think that finding out what your credit score is would be easy. In a way it is, but only because I've done my research and you won't have to spend time surfing websites looking for the ever-elusive credit number. It would seem logical to have your credit score appear right on your credit report, but that's just not the way it is.

At one time, your credit score was a big secret known only to financial companies and banks. With the **FACT ACT,** legislators decided that it was important for individuals to know not only what their personal credit scores are but how they are calculated and how to improve them.

The main company who calculates your credit score is the Field, Isaac Company commonly known as FICO. They invented the concept of the FICO scores so they are the ones who are known as experts in the industry. Before we go into finding your score, let's look at a few facts about the FICO score.

- FICO scores are your credit rating
- They range from 300-850, higher is better

- Most lenders base approval on them
- Higher scores mean lower interest rates
- FICO scores are calculated based on your rating in five general categories:

    Payment history - 35%

    Amounts owed - 30%

    Length of credit history - 15%

    New credit - 10%

    Types of credit used - 10%

Isaac Company is the inventor the FICO score

- They have the only website offering all 3 of your FICO scores
- The median FICO score in the U.S. 723

Essentially, your credit score is simply a snapshot of your credit use -- it's the Cliffs Notes version of seven years of your borrowing history. In many lending situations, the lender bases its decision almost solely on your credit score. Consider your credit score the overall GPA of your borrowing history.

Now, here's the bad news. If you want to know your actual credit score, you will usually have to purchase it. This can be done in a few ways.

You can get it from one of the three major credit reporting companies: Equifax, Experian, and

TransUnion. The fee isn't a huge one – usually around $15 or $20. However, if you're serious about growing your credit score, it's well worth the money to be financially responsible in the end.

You can also go to www.myfico.com and get your FICO score directly from them. They will offer you a free 30 day trial membership which will get your credit score right now and then, if you wish to continue the membership, it will update the score as it rises or lowers.

If you are applying for a mortgage, here's a little good news for you. You can find out your credit score for free! The mortgage company will base their decision and interest rate on what your credit score number is, so just ask and they'll tell you!

FICO scores range between 300 and 850. Here's what those scores mean:

- Over 750 - you have excellent credit and will be able obtain credit easily

- 720 or more - you still have very good credit and will be able to obtain credit easily

- 660 to 720 - this is an acceptable credit. You can still get loans, but you may pay a higher interest rate

- 620 to 660 - creditors are going to be uncertain about lending you money

- Less than 620 - you have poor credit history and will probably not be able to obtain credit on your own

Knowing the above information makes it obvious that if you need or want to get credit for something, the higher your score is, the better your chances are to not only get credit but get it at a handsome interest rate. If you are in the 660 to 620 range, you may still get a loan, but the interest rate is likely to be higher.

That's why it's important to keep your credit good or establish good credit from the get go. That's where we'll start.

Establishing Good Credit

So, you don't have any credit to speak of, but you have big plans for the future. Maybe you're a fresh college graduate or a young person eager to buy your first new car.

If you have never had to use credit before, first of all BRAVO! Of course, it's best to pay cash for the things you need so that you don't have to worry about credit card payments, loan payments, or interest rates.

But if you're young, the chances of you needing credit in the future are very real. Someday you might want to buy a house. Perhaps you'll want to buy a new car.

Chances are pretty good that you won't have the cash outright to buy these high ticket items which mean you'll need credit. Plus, it's always good to have a little credit since many utility companies will look at your credit to turn on your power bill, for example, without a deposit of some type.

When you're starting fresh with no credit history at all, here are a few ways to get a good start on establishing good credit:

1. Pay your bills on time especially mortgage or rent payments. Apart from extreme circumstances like bankruptcy or tax liens, nothing has as big of an impact on your credit history as late payments.

2. Establish credit early. Having clean, active charge accounts established many years ago will boost your score in ways you will be proud of yourself. If you are averse to credit, on principle, consider setting up automatic monthly payments for, say, utilities and phone on a credit card account and locking the card away where it's not a temptation.

3. Don't max out available credit on credit card accounts. Lenders won't be impressed. Instead, they are much more likely to assume that you have trouble managing your finances. Beyond one or two credit cards, it starts to get complicated.

4. Don't apply for too much credit in short amount of time. Multiple requests for your credit history (not including requests by you to check your file) will reduce your score. If you are hunting around for good loan rates, assume that every time you give your Social Security number to a lender or credit card company, they will order a credit history.

5. Be neat and consistent when filling out applications. This ensure that all your good deeds get recorded in a single file, as opposed to multiple files or, worse, someone else's file. Watch out for inconsistencies in use of "Jr." and "Sr."

6. Check your credit history for errors especially if you will requesting a time-dependent loan, like a mortgage.

One great way to start establishing credit is to apply for a store credit card (Sears, JC Penney, etc.). Once you get the card, make a few small purchases and pay them off completely. Do this a few times over the course of a year and you'll find yourself with some established credit with an excellent payment history. DO NOT go overboard and buy more than what you can pay for, though.

You can also apply for a secured credit card. These cards ask that you place a certain amount of money in your account for which you will receive a charge card. Then you can make purchases up to the amount of money that is in your account. Credit reporting agencies treat these cards just like regular credit cards and look to them as a responsible way for you to establish a good credit history.

You will have to have a checking account to establish credit. This lends to your credibility with lenders and shows that you are able to manage your money effectively.

When applying for a credit card of any type, be sure to ask if they report to any of the credit reporting agencies. As we've said before, they are not required to do so, and if they don't, having one of these cards or loans won't do you a lick of good even if you do make your payments on time.

You can also establish credit by making a purchase or applying for a loan with a co-signer. A co-signer is a person with good credit history who is basically telling the lending company that they will be responsible for making sure you make your payments on time. Often a co-signer is a relative such as a parent. This can be a risky proposition for them, so know that they are putting their own credit history on the line just to help you out, so don't let them down.

When applying for a loan, such as a car loan, it can also be helpful if you have a large down payment to make thus lessening the amount of money you have to borrow. This shows the lending company that you have the ability to save and they are more likely to take a chance on you based on this factor alone.

Let's do a quick review on how to establish a good credit history:

- Apply for a store or gas credit card and make a few charges
- Ask a loved one to co-sign on a loan
- Find a respected secured credit card company
- Open a checking account

- Don't apply for too many credit cards in too short of a time
- Check your credit report for any errors
- Go slowly
- Don't overspend
- Make sure your lender reports to at least one of the credit reporting agencies
- MAKE YOUR PAYMENTS ON TIME!!!!!!!

Of course, the last one is the most important in establishing credit. If you don't make your payments on time, it won't make a hill of beans worth of difference what you are trying to do. This is what makes your credit history worthwhile – making on time payments and showing you are responsible with your credit and your creditors.

So, what if you've already had credit, but you've made some mistakes over the years finding yourself with bad credit? Is all hope lost? The good news is – NO!

Jeni Temen

Repairing Your Credit Score

Don't despair if you find yourself with a less than desirable credit score and credit history. You are human and can make mistakes. It's natural. The key to this is recognize that your spending habits are out of control, your credit has been damaged, and then vow to never get yourself back in the same situation after you have gotten your credit repaired.

First, get your credit report. Get one from all three agencies. You get one free and then you'll probably have to pay around $10 a piece for the other two. It's important to get reports from all three agencies so that you have a full picture of your credit history.

Some companies only report to one agency. Some report to all three. But if you are committed to repairing your credit, you need all three so that you don't miss anything.

Then go over those credit reports carefully. See the section above on how to read these credit reports. Check to see that there are no errors such as a bill you've paid but that is still being shown as owed.

People at credit bureaus are human too and make mistakes just like you! If you don't call attention to these mistakes, no one else will. We'll cover correcting those mistakes a little bit later.

The next part involves pulling out those accounts that are delinquent and making a re-payment plan. Unless you are declaring bankruptcy, you'll still need to pay your debts and doing so can go a long way towards improving your credit history. Creditors will see that you are doing the best you can to get back on your feet and this will improve your credibility.

If all the bills are too overwhelming for you to consider paying back at once, just concentrate on one at a time. Break them into pieces, contact the company and let them know you are trying to come up with a repayment plan and if there's anything they can do to help you out.

These companies really just want their money in the long run, so they are going to be willing to help you. Once that company is paid off, move on to the next one until everyone is paid off.

After that happens, it's not like your credit is immediately pristine. Late payments and charged-off accounts remain on your report for seven years; bankruptcies for 10.

Most creditors, however, look for a pattern of payment rather than focusing on one-time or rare occurrences. That's why consistent on-time bill payments will improve those blemishes.

As soon as you have paid off your creditors, then you can start all over again. Follow the steps given above in the section about establishing credit. Nothing can compare to consistent, on-time bill payments and responsible credit practices when it comes to repairing your credit.

Experts say the average time required to rebuild one's credit to the point at which you can be accepted for a major credit card or small loan is approximately two years.

Here are some other things to consider when trying to repair your credit:

> • Pay down your credit cards. Paying off your installment loans (mortgage, auto, student, etc.) can help your score, but typically not as dramatically as paying down -- or paying off -- revolving accounts like credit cards.

The credit-scoring formulas like to see a nice, big gap between the amount of credit you're using and your available credit limits. Getting your balances below 30% of the credit limit on each card can really help.

While most debt gurus recommend paying off the highest-rate card first, a better strategy here is to pay down the cards that are closest to their limits.

> • Use your cards lightly. Racking up big balances can hurt your score, regardless of whether you pay your bill in full each month.

What's typically reported to the credit bureaus, and thus calculated into your score, is the balance reported on your last statement. That doesn't mean paying off your balances each month isn't financially smart -- it is -- just that the credit score doesn't care.

You typically can increase your score by limiting your charges to 30% or less of a card's limit. If you're having trouble keeping track, consider using a check register to track your spending, logging into your account frequently at the issuer's Web site, or using personal finance software like Microsoft Money or Quicken, which can download your transactions and balances automatically.

> • Check your limits. Your score might be artificially depressed if your lender is showing a lower limit than you've actually got. Most credit-card issuers will quickly update this information if you ask.

If your issuer makes it a policy not to report consumers' limits, however -- as is the usual case with American Express cards and those issued by

Capital One -- the bureaus typically use your highest balance as a proxy for your credit limit.

You may see the problem here: If you consistently charge the same amount each month -- say $2,000 to $2,500 -- it may look to the credit-scoring formula like you're regularly maxing out that card.

You could go on a wild spending spree to raise the limit, but a more sober solution would simply be to pay your balance down or off before your statement period closes.

Check your last statement to see which day of the month that typically is, then go to the issuer's Web site about a week in advance of closing and pay off what you owe. It won't raise your reported limit, but it will widen the gap between that limit and your closing balance, which should boost your score.

> • Dust off an old card. The older your credit history, the better. But if you stop using your oldest cards, the issuers may stop updating those accounts at the credit bureaus. The accounts will still appear, but they won't be given as much weight in the credit-scoring formula as your active accounts. That's why many financial companies recommend to their clients that they use their oldest cards every few months to charge a small amount, paying it off in full when the statement arrives.

- Get some goodwill. If you've been a good customer, a lender might agree to simply erase that one late payment from your credit history. You usually have to make the request in writing, and your chances for a "goodwill adjustment" improve the better your record with the company (and the better your credit in general). But it can't hurt to ask.

A longer-term solution for more-troubled accounts is to ask that they be "re- aged." If the account is still open, the lender might erase previous submissions.

When trying to improve your credit score or credit history, avoid any of the following:

- Asking a creditor to lower your credit limits This will reduce that important gap between your balances and your available credit, which could hurt your score. If a lender asks you to close an account or get a limit lowered as a condition for getting a loan, you might have to do it -- but don't do so without being asked.

- Making a late payment. The irony here is that .a late or missed payment will hurt a good score more than a bad one, dropping a 700-plus score by 100 points or more. If you've already got a string of negative items on your credit report, one more won't have a big impact, but it's still something you want to avoid if you're trying to improve your score.

- Consolidating your accounts. Applying for a new account can ding your score. So, too, can transferring balances from a high-limit card to a lower- limit one, or concentrating all or most of your credit-card balances onto a single card. In general, it's better to have smaller balances on a few cards than a big balance on one.

- Applying for new credit if you've already got plenty. On the other hand, applying for, and getting an installment loan can help your score if you don't have any installment accounts, or you're trying to recover from a credit disaster like bankruptcy.

By the way, all these suggestions work best if you have poor or mediocre scores to begin with. Once you've hit the 700 mark, any tweaking you do will tend to have less of a positive impact. And if your scores are in the "excellent" category, 760 or above, you'll probably be able to eke out only a few extra points despite your best efforts. There's really no point, anyway, since you're already qualified for the best rates and terms. Here's one area where it's really OK to rest on your laurels and worry about something else.

If you are in serious, serious credit problems, sometimes the only solution is to file for a bankruptcy. This is a last-ditch thing, though, and should only be done if you've dug yourself in so deep that the odds of getting out of debt are little to none.

Bankruptcy

Filing for bankruptcy has a very negative connotation in society, but it's a way for people who have found themselves in serious financial trouble to ease the burden of what they've done and allow them to start over. Businesses don't like it, but for consumers, it can be a life saver.

This writer knows of one young girl – just 21 years old – who was over $20,000 in debt plus she had her car repossessed for non-payment. At this young age, she was in serious financial trouble with no way out.

She was (still is) going to school trying to earn a degree so she can get a good job, but since her first credit card was issued to her at age 17, her credit woes began and they didn't end until she was able to file for bankruptcy.

Her debts were discharged and she was able to start all over again. She purchased a (very) used vehicle for cash, got a part-time job while she went to school and worked very hard to build her credit up slowly.

Now she is 30. She has a well-paying job as a nurse at a local hospital and just celebrated buying her first home. She once told me, "I knew I was in over my head and I became very depressed because of it. The bankruptcy was the best thing I could have ever done for myself even though at the time, it was the hardest."

Let's start by exploring the different types of bankruptcies. There are three different filings you can make: Chapter 7, Chapter 11, and Chapter 13.

Chapter 7 Bankruptcy

Chapter 7 bankruptcy: sometimes call a straight bankruptcy is a liquidation proceeding. The debtor turns over all non-exempt property to the bankruptcy trustee who then converts it to cash for distribution to the creditors.

The debtor receives a discharge of all dischargeable debts usually within four months. In the vast majority of cases the debtor has no assets that he would lose so Chapter 7 will give that person a relatively quick "fresh start".

One of the main purposes of Bankruptcy Law is to give a person, who is hopelessly burdened with debt, a fresh start by wiping out his or her debts.

New legislation has been passed regarding Chapter 7 bankruptcies. Laws can vary from state to state, so you will want to check with someone who knows or do extensive research as to what is allowed to be discharged with a Chapter 7 and what is not in your state.

Essentially what the new laws ask of people who are filing a Chapter 7 bankruptcy is twofold. First, they must take an approved credit counseling course within six months before filing. They must also complete an approved financial management course before any debts can be discharged.

Even though those two new stipulations are in place, it is still relatively easy to file for a Chapter 7 bankruptcy. There are, of course, governmental "hoops" you will have to jump through which is why it is often a good idea to secure the services of a bankruptcy lawyer. However, it is possible for you to do this yourself as long as you do your research and "cross your T's and dot your I's"!

What are the most common reasons given for filing a Chapter 7 bankruptcy? Well, of course, it's the accumulation of excessive debt! But seriously, here are the most common reasons why people get into such debt:

- Medical bills
- Unemployment
- Divorce
- Overextended credit
- Large, unexpected expense

A Harvard Study reported that half of US bankruptcies were caused by medical bills. The study was published online in February of 2005 by Health Affairs. The Harvard study concluded that illness and medical bills caused half (50.4 percent) of the 1,458,000 personal bankruptcies in 2001. The study estimates that medical bankruptcies affect about 2 million Americans annually — counting debtors and their dependents, including about 700,000 children.

If you find that you have to file for a Chapter 7 bankruptcy, you may be worried about whether or not you'll get to keep some of the things that are important to you and essential to life. These things include a car and your home, among other things.

Unsecured debts, such as credit card debt, personal loans, money judgments and certain taxes are wiped out in a Chapter 7. However, certain debts are not dischargeable under Chapter 7 bankruptcy; these debts include, but are not limited to, most student loans, certain taxes, alimony and child or other court ordered support payments.

If a debt is secured by property, such as a home mortgage or an automobile loan, then you get to decide how to handle that debt. For example, in the case of a vehicle, you could:

1. Keep the automobile and the debt as long as you are current and continue keep your payments current

2. "Redeem" the automobile which means pay it off at its current "fair market value"

3. Return the vehicle, include any balance due in your bankruptcy and pay nothing further on the vehicle. The choice is yours.

In 99% of the Chapter 7 cases, the person filing bankruptcy keeps all of their property. Bankruptcy law is not meant to punish you and allows you to keep your property under what are called "exemptions" or things you get to keep. You keep your car, your house, your jewelry, the boat, your clothing, everything!

Of course, if you still owe a debt on anything like your car and your house, you should refer to the above scenario. If you want to discharge your car loan, you'll have to either pay up or give up the car.

Chapter 13 Bankruptcy

Another option for bankruptcy for individuals is the Chapter 13. This is more commonly known as a reorganization bankruptcy. Chapter13 bankruptcy is filed by individuals who want to pay off their debts over a period of three to five years.

This type of bankruptcy appeals to individuals who have non-exempt property that they want to keep. It is also only an option for individuals who have predictable income and whose income is sufficient to pay their reasonable expenses with some amount left over to pay off their debts.

There are many reasons why people choose Chapter 13 bankruptcy instead of Chapter 7 bankruptcy. Generally, you are probably a good candidate for Chapter 13 bankruptcy if you are in any of the following situations:

1. You have a sincere desire to repay your debts, but you need the protection of the bankruptcy court to do so. You may think filing Chapter 13 bankruptcy is simply the "Right Thing To Do" rather than file Chapter 7.

2. You are behind on your mortgage or car loan and want to make up the missed payments over time

and reinstate the original agreement. You cannot do this in Chapter 7 bankruptcy. You can make up missed payments only in Chapter 13 bankruptcy.

3. You need help repaying your debts now but need to leave open the option of filing for Chapter 7 bankruptcy in the future. This would be the case if for some reason you can't stop incurring new debt.

4. You are a family farmer who wants to pay off your debts, but you do not qualify for a Chapter 12 family farming bankruptcy because you have a large debt unrelated to farming.

5. You have valuable nonexempt property. When you file for Chapter 7 bankruptcy, you get to keep certain property, called exempt. If you have a lot of nonexempt property (which you'd have to give up if you file a Chapter 7 bankruptcy), Chapter 13 bankruptcy may be the better option.

6. You received a Chapter 7 discharge within the previous eight years. You cannot file for Chapter 7 again until the eight years are up.

A Chapter 13 can be filed if:

- The debtor received a discharge under Chapter 7, 11, or 12, more than four years ago.

- The debtor received a discharge under Chapter 13 more than two years ago.

- You have a co-debtor on a personal debt, if you file for Chapter 7 bankruptcy, your creditor will go after the co-debtor for payment. If you file for Chapter 13 bankruptcy, the creditor will leave your co-debtor alone, as long as you keep up with your bankruptcy plan payments.

- You have a tax debt. If large part of your debt consists of federal taxes, what happens to your tax debts may determine which type of bankruptcy is best for you.

As of October 17, 2005, new bankruptcy laws took effect for all three types of bankruptcy. When it comes to Chapter 13, you cannot file this way unless the following conditions are met:

- The debtor received a discharge under Chapter 7, 11 or 12 more than four years ago

- The debtor received a discharge under Chapter 13 more than two years ago.

- When a motor vehicle was purchased within 910 days (2 1/2 years) the filing and a secured creditor has a lien on it, the creditor retains the lien until payment of the entire debt has been made.

The following debt is NOT discharged:

- taxes for which returns were never filed or filed late (within two years of the petition date);

- taxes for which the debtor made a fraudulent return or evaded taxes
- domestic support payments
- Student loans
- Drunk driving injuries
- Criminal restitution
- Civil restitutions or damages awarded for willful or malicious personal actions causing personal injury or death.

- All tax returns the four years prior to filling Chapter 13 must be filed.

- Debtors must provide to the trustee, at least seven days prior to the 341 meeting, a copy of a tax return or transcript of a tax return, for the period for which the return was most recently due

Chapter 11 Bankruptcy

A Chapter 11 bankruptcy is filed by businesses and is quite similar to a Chapter 13. A Chapter 11 is available for individuals, but it is generally used by businesses to reorganize their debts and dealings so that they can be more financially solid.

When a troubled business is unable to service its debt or pay its creditors, they can file with a federal bankruptcy court for protection under either a Chapter 7 or a Chapter 11 bankruptcy.

In a Chapter 7 bankruptcy, the business must cease operation and a trustee will sell all its assets and distribute the proceeds to the business's creditors ratably in accordance with statutory priorities.

A Chapter 11 filing, on the other hand, is usually filed in an attempt to stay in business while a bankruptcy court supervises the reorganization of the company's contractual and debt obligations. The court can grant complete or partial relief from most of the company's debts along with its contracts so that the company can make a fresh start.

Often, if the company's debts exceed its assets, then at the completion of the bankruptcy, the company's owners or stockholders all end up with nothing. All their rights and interests are terminated and the company's creditors end up with ownership of the newly reorganized company in the hopes that it will eventually succeed financially as compensation for their losses.

So, in general, an individual bankruptcy will be under a Chapter 7 or Chapter 11. It's a big decision for you to make, but sometimes, it's the only way you can "get out from under" and begin anew.

Before you resort to filing for a Chapter 7 or Chapter 11, consider the alternatives. Creditors might be willing to settle their claim for a smaller cash payment, or they might be willing to stretch out the loan and reduce the size of the payments. This would allow you to pay off the debt by making smaller payments over a longer period of time. The creditor would eventually receive the full economic benefit of its bargain.

Occasionally, you may "buy time" by consolidating your debts; that is, by taking out a big loan to pay off all the smaller amounts of debts that you owe. The primary danger of this approach is that it is very easy to go out and use your credit cards to borrow even more.

In that case, you end up with an even larger total debt and no more income to meet the monthly payments. Indeed, if you have taken out a second mortgage on your home to obtain the consolidation loan, you might lose your home as well. When there really is no other way out, you'll need to file for a Chapter 7 personal bankruptcy. Try looking at it in a positive light, however.

There are some advantages to filing for bankruptcy. By far the most important advantage is that debtors may obtain a fresh financial start. Consumers who are eligible for Chapter 7 may be forgiven (discharged from) most unsecured debts.

A secured debt is one which the creditor is entitled to collect by seizing and selling certain assets of the debtor if payments are missed, such as a home mortgage or car loan. With those two major exceptions, most consumer debts are unsecured. You may be able to keep (that is, exempt) many of your assets, although state laws vary widely in defining which assets you may keep.

Collection efforts must stop as soon as you file for bankruptcy under Chapter 7 or Chapter 13. As soon as your petition is filed, there is by law an automatic stay, which prohibits most collection activity. If a creditor continues to try to collect the debt, the creditor may be cited for contempt of court or ordered to pay damages. The stay applies even to the loan that you may have obtained to buy your car.

If you continue to make payments, it is unlikely that your creditor will do anything. However, if you miss payments your creditor will probably petition to have the stay lifted in order either to repossess the car or to renegotiate the loan. You cannot be fired from your job solely because you filed for bankruptcy.

Of course, there are disadvantages to filing for bankruptcy. Since your bankruptcy filing will remain on your credit record for up to ten years, it may affect your future finances. A bankruptcy is a troublesome item in your credit record, but often debtors who file already have a troublesome history.

In one respect, bankruptcy may improve your credit records. Because Chapter 7 provides for a discharge of debts no more than once every eight years, lenders know that a credit applicant who has just emerged from Chapter 7 cannot soon repeat the process.

Research in this area has produced mixed results. A study by the Credit Research Center at Purdue University found that about one-third of consumers who filed for bankruptcy had obtained lines of credit within three years of filing; one-half had obtained them within five years. However, the new credit itself may reflect the record of bankruptcy. For example, if you might have been eligible for a bank card with a 14 percent rate before bankruptcy, the best card that you can get after bankruptcy might carry a rate of 20 percent—or you might have to rely on a card secured by a deposit that you make with the credit card issuer.

There are a couple of ways you can go about filing for bankruptcy. The most reliable is to secure a bankruptcy attorney and have them do it for you. They are experts in this area and will often take care of everything for you including appearing in court on your behalf. They do charge a fee for this service, however. That fee can range anywhere from $500 to $2,000 depending on your area. Yes, it is odd that they'll charge that high a fee to file a bankruptcy for someone who doesn't have money in the first place, but many will accept payments.

You can also file the bankruptcy yourself. There are many places on the Internet where you can download the forms you will need. Be advised that they are often lengthy and in-depth, but they are fairly straight-forward when you take the time to fill them out completely.

Once you have the forms all filled out, take them to your local courthouse and pay the filing fee which is usually around $100 to $200. You will receive a notice of a court date at which time you will need to show up and the judge will grant your request for bankruptcy.

The bad part about filing yourself is that you have to contact all your creditors yourself to let them know that the bankruptcy has been filed. You have to be very careful to list each and every one of your debts so they will apply under the discharge order.

If you miss even one, you will have to pay it after the bankruptcy is granted.

Filing for bankruptcy might not be your only option. One of the newest trends in achieving financial freedom and a good credit score is to secure the services of a credit counseling or debt consolidation company. But do they work?

Credit Counselors and Debt Consolidators

These companies have started popping up everywhere. In fact, as I am writing this book, there is a commercial on television for yet another credit counseling company. It seems like they are everywhere. It also seems like they can really help you with your debt problems. But can they?

There are some credit counseling agencies and debt consolidators that can actually, help get people out of debt. But there are also others who are simply trying to get money (that you don't have) without helping you at all.

There is a difference between these two types of companies. Credit counselors will help you get out of debt and stay out of debt. That means that they will help you realize where you went wrong on the financial road and then help you get out of debt. After that, they will put you on a budget and offer services that can help you stay out of debt and live a financially stable life.

Debt consolidation companies are different, though not entirely. They also will help you get out of debt, but they do so by working with your creditors to help combine all of your debts into one large debt with one monthly payment. That usually entails getting some type of loan on your behalf that will pay off your creditors and you will pay the loan company instead.

Because of the services they provide, many people would rather go with a credit counseling service. That's because they need someone to help them stay away from the mindset that got them into debt in the first place. There are many, many credit counseling companies out there.

What do you need to look for in a reputable credit counseling company?

Here are a few suggestions:

> • They should be associated with the Better Business Bureau. The service's website should have a BBB logo and a link to their record on the Better Business Bureau website. Click through the link to check that there are no unresolved complaints against them.

Many people only think about the Better Business Bureau after they've been cheated, but by then there's not much you can do. Working with a credit counseling agency that is a member of the Better Business Bureau means that you can go to them to help mediate any dispute you might have with the service provider.

- Reputable credit counseling services will be accredited by an independent nonprofit, just as many schools are. One such accreditation body is the National Institute for Financial Counseling Education.

- A good credit counseling agency will charge a small, reasonable monthly fee, usually around $30. Some also charge a fee upfront, though this fee should be reasonable (around $50 tops). It may be possible to get a hardship waiver of these fees if you truly do not have the $30-50.

- You will have to fill out an application when you decide to go with a credit counseling agency. The application must clearly say what the fees to be paid are, what the services to be provided are, and in what timeframe all of this will be provided.

- Run far, far away from any organization that proposes to "wipe out" your debt for you, rather than simply helping you to repay the debt. Short of your creditors just deciding to forget about the debt (unlikely), there is no way to erase debt—even bankruptcy leaves a huge mark on your credit report for ten years.

True, your car may not go missing from your driveway if you stop paying unsecured debt (i.e., debt that is not "secured" with collateral, like most credit cards, unlike most auto loans). But you are still legally obligated to pay the debt, and the possibility of being taken to court will loom over you. You will likely be unable to get even "bad credit" financing if you still have debts in collections–good luck buying a car or house.

Now let's look at how a reputable credit counseling service will work. First, they will negotiate with your creditors to establish a debt management plan (DMP) for you. A DMP may help the debtor repay his or her debt by working out a repayment plan with the creditor. DMPs, set up by credit counselors, usually offer reduced payments, fees and interest rates to the client. Credit counselors refer to the terms dictated by the creditors to determine payments or interest reductions offered to consumers in a debt management plan.

After joining a DMP, the creditors will close the customer's accounts and restrict the accounts to future charges. The most common benefit of a DMP as advertised by most agencies is the consolidation of multiple monthly payments into just one monthly payment which is usually less than the sum of the individual payment previously paid by the customer.

This is because the credit card banks will usually accept a lower monthly payment from a customer in a DMP than if the customer were paying the account on their own. Some DMPs advertise that payments can be cut by 50 % although a reduction of 10 to 20 percent is more common.

The second feature of a DMP is a reduction in interest rates charged by creditors. A customer with a defaulted credit card account will often be paying an interest rate approaching 30 percent. Upon joining a DMP, credit card banks sometimes lower the annual percentage rates charged to 5 to 10 percent and a few will eliminate the interest altogether.

This reduction in interest allows the counseling agencies to advertise that their customers will be debt free in periods of three to six years rather than the twenty plus years that it would take to pay off a large amount of debt at high interest rates. That's a very attractive advantage – especially for people who are in debt quite a bit.

A third benefit offered by credit counseling agencies is the process of bringing delinquent accounts current. This is often called "re-aging" or "curing" an account. This usually occurs after making a series of on-time payments through the DMP as a show of good faith and commitment to completion of the program.

For example, a client with an account that has a monthly payment of $50 but that monthly payment has not been paid in two months might be considered by the creditor to be 60 days past due. After joining the DMP and making three consecutive on-time monthly payments, the creditor could "re-age" the account to reflect a current status.

After that, the monthly payment due on the statements would be the monthly payment negotiated by the DMP and the account would be reported as current to the credit bureaus. Now this process does not eliminate the prior delinquencies from the credit reports.

What is does is merely give a fresh start and opportunity for the client to begin building a positive credit history. Like all negative credit information, only the passage of time will lessen the impact of the negative marks when credit scores are calculated.

So how do credit counseling companies make money? They do charge a fee to you for their services, and it is important for you to get all of that information in writing before you sign on the dotted line. However, this fee is not usually enough to make them a huge profit.

The credit counseling companies make most of their compensation from the creditors to whom the debt payments are distributed. This funding relationship has led many to believe that credit counseling agencies are merely a collections wing of the creditors.

This fee income, known as "Fair Share," consists of contributions from the creditors that originally earned the agency 15% of the amount recovered. However, in recent years, Fair Share contributions have dwindled steadily, with contributions of 4-10% being the most common.

There is a lot of criticism, in fact, when it comes to credit counseling agencies and their effectiveness as well as legality. The Federal Trade Commission has filed lawsuits against several credit counseling agencies, and they continue to urge caution to consumers when it comes to choosing a credit counseling agency.

The FTC has received over 8,000 complaints from consumers about shady credit counselors. Many of those complaints concern high or hidden fees along with the inability to opt out of so-called "voluntary" contributions. The Better Business Bureau also reports high complaint levels about credit counseling.

Not surprisingly, the IRS has also weighed in on the subject of credit counseling and has denied non-profit, tax-exempt status to around thirty of the nation's 1,000 credit counseling agencies. Those thirty agencies account for more
than half of the industry's revenue. Audits of non-profit credit counseling agencies by the IRS are ongoing.

The lobby against credit counselors arises from the belief by the collection industry that the not-for-profit status of the credit counselors gives them an unfair financial and market advantage over them. The IRS apparently agrees.

The tax exempt revocations seem to be centered on whether or not a tax exempt credit counselor actually performed their mandated mission by assisting the community at large as opposed to offering their whole attention to their own DMP customers in a "collection practice". However, that has yet to be proven.

Congress has also investigated the credit counseling industry and has issued a report that says while some agencies are ethical, others charge excessive fees and provide poor service to consumers. The report also states that NFCC member guidelines, if applied to the entire industry, would go a long way toward eliminating the abuses they have uncovered in other parts of the industry.

When it comes to debt consolidation companies, you are talking about an entirely different concept. What a debt consolidation company does is negotiate with creditors to get a lower pay-off amount for your debts and then obtain a loan on your behalf to pay off those creditors allowing you to make just one payment instead of multiple ones.

The two types of companies are similar in nature, but with debt consolidation, the only thing they do is negotiate with credit lenders and then get you one payment instead of many. They do charge a fee for their services as well just as the credit counseling companies do.

The thing about debt consolidation companies is that they do what you can do yourself with just a little bit of work. You can call your creditors and negotiate a pay-off balance for your accounts and then obtain your own loan as a debt consolidation loan. Even if you have less than perfect credit, most banks and lending institutions will have debt consolidation loans available to almost everyone.

Really, the bottom line when considering either a debt consolidation company or a credit counselor is to weight the advantages and disadvantages first. Then check out the company you are considering to make sure they are reputable.

These types of companies can really and truly help people who are seriously in debt. But proceed with caution and choose wisely lest you get yourself involved in yet another problem besides your debt!

Now that we've addressed no credit, bad credit, and people who can help with credit problems, let's focus on your credit report and your credit score. Often, there are mistakes that are on your credit report, and correcting them is essential.

Mistakes Can Be Made

As we've said before, your credit report is very important to you as well as your credit score. People are human and the information contained in your credit report is entered in by human hands. Sometimes those hands make mistakes.

Maybe you paid off a past due bill and it's still showing on your credit report as delinquent. There are all sorts of things that can be reflected incorrectly on your credit report, so it's important that you take steps to make corrections as soon as you can.

The first thing you need to do is check over your report and dispute any old negative reports you can find. Say that fight with your phone company over an unfair bill a few years ago resulted in a collections account. You can continue protesting that the charge was unjust, or you can try disputing the account with the credit bureaus as "not mine."

The older and smaller a collection account, the more likely the collection agency won't bother to verify it when the credit bureau investigates your dispute. Some consumers also have had luck disputing old items with a lender that has merged with another company, which can leave lender records a real mess.

If there are significant errors on your credit report, you need to be sure and get them removed right away. However, there are also some mistakes that you can ignore and it won't impact you negatively.

Your credit score is calculated based on the information in your credit report, so certain errors there can really cost you. But not everything that's reported in your file matters to your score.

Here's the stuff that's usually worth the effort of correcting with the bureaus:

- Late payments, charge-offs, collections or negative items that aren't yours.

- Credit reported as lower than they actually are.

- Accounts listed as "settled", "paid derogatory," "paid charge-offs", or anything other than "current" or "paid as agreed" if you paid on time and in full.

- Accounts that are listed as unpaid that were included in a bankruptcy.

- Negative items older than seven years (10 in case of bankruptcy) that should have automatically fallen off your report.

You actually have to be a bit careful with this last one, because sometimes scores actually go down when bad items fall off your report. It's a quirk in the FICO credit-scoring software, and the potential effect of eliminating old negative items is difficult to predict in advance.

Some of the stuff that you typically shouldn't worry about includes:

- Various misspellings your name.
- Outdated or incorrect address.
- An old employer listed as current.
- Most inquiries.

If the misspelled name or incorrect address is because of identity theft or because your file has been mixed with someone else's, that should be obvious when you look at your accounts. You'll see delinquencies or accounts that aren't yours and should report that immediately. However, if it's just a goof by the credit bureau or one of the companies reporting to it, it's usually not much to sweat about.

Two more items you don't need to correct:

- Accounts you closed listed as open.
- Accounts you closed that say, "closed by consumer."

Closing accounts can't help your score and may hurt it. If your goal is boosting your score, leave these alone. Once an account has been closed, though, it doesn't matter to the scoring formulas that did it -- you or the lender. If you messed up the account, it will be obvious from the late payments and other derogatory information included in the file.

Say you've found some significant errors on your credit report and you need to correct them. There are certain steps you need to take in order to make sure, that the error is corrected and ultimately removed from your report.

1. Make a copy of your credit report and circle every item you believe is incorrect.

2. Write a letter to the reporting agency (the address will be printed on the report). Explain each dispute and request an investigation to resolve the issues. If you have supporting paperwork, send it along, coding pages to match dispute paragraphs. Do not send your originals.

3. Send all materials by certified mail, return receipt requested so that you can prove the packet was received.

4. Send a similar letter of dispute to the creditor whose reporting statements you disagree with. Refer to a billing statement to find the correct address for disputes, because it's usually different from the payment address. If your dispute involves personal information, such as your current address, enclose

a copy of your driver's license or a utility bill in your name to verify your residence.

The reporting agency will initiate an investigation, contacting your creditors to verify the accuracy of the information. If the creditor cannot verify that the entry is correct, it must be removed. When the investigation is complete, the agency must send you a free copy of your report if changes were made.

If the investigation uncovers an error, you have the right to ask that a corrected version of your credit report be sent to everyone who received the report during the past six months.

It's a good idea to contact your creditor first, then allow a bit of lead time before you submit the dispute to the reporting agency. By the time the dispute is verified, the creditor will hopefully have corrected the error.

You can also make changes online directly with the credit reporting agency. When you are on their website, they will usually have links that allow you to click a button to dispute incorrect information.

You can initiate an investigation from many online credit reports by following the links provided and checking the disputed items as directed. There sometimes isn't a place for remarks--you'll simply check a multiple-choice reason for each dispute.

If the credit reporting agency says the original information is accurate, it must provide you with a written notice that includes the name, address, and phone number of the person who made the report. If you still disagree, initiate a second investigation.

Unfortunately, in the real world the reporting agencies often try to sidestep that requirement, giving you standard, computer-generated information rather than the facts you need to find the person or department who made the negative report.
Keep plugging away until you have the answer you're looking for.

If your attempts to correct an entry are unsuccessful, you can ask the reporting agency to insert a 100-character explanation next to it that explains your side of the story.

Under the Fair Credit Reporting Act, the credit bureau is required to solve the problem in a reasonable amount of time, generally 30 days. If you feel that a credit bureau has not responded promptly and fairly to your situation, contact the attorney general of your state or the Federal Trade Commission in Washington at 202-FTC-HELP.

If you are disputing something on your credit report, you might want to try the following sample letter in your attempts:

Date
Your Name
Your Address
Your City, State, Zip Code

Complaint Department
Name of Company
Address
City, State, Zip Code

Dear Sir or Madam:

I am writing to dispute the following information in my file. The items I dispute also are encircled on the attached copy of the report I received.

This item (identify item(s) disputed by name of source, such as creditors or tax court, and identify type of item, such as credit account, judgment, etc.) is (inaccurate or incomplete) because (describe what is inaccurate or incomplete and why). I am requesting that the item be deleted (or request another specific change) to correct the information.

Enclosed are copies of (use this sentence if applicable and describe any enclosed documentation, such as payment records, court documents) supporting my position. Please investigate this (these) matter(s) and (delete or correct) the disputed item(s) as soon as possible.

Sincerely,

Your name

Enclosures: (List what you are enclosing)

Identity Theft And Your Credit

Another great reason for keeping tabs on your credit report as much as possible is the possibility of identity theft. It happens all the time and often the only way you'll know it has happened to you is to check your credit report.

Criminals know the way to steal your identity, and the worst part is that it's not all that difficult. You know all those credit card applications you get in the mail? If you don't shred them, they can use that to steal your identity.

It's not above them to sift through garbage just to obtain a social security number or a driver's license number. Once they have these vital bits of information, it's easy for them to steal your identity.

What they will do is scary. They will apply for credit cards in your name and max them out within days. They will obtain loans in your name and never make a payment. Then the loan company comes after you for the money. It's something that affects millions and millions of people each year and it can be a real mess when it comes to your credit report.

As many as 85 percent of all identity theft victims find out about the crime only when they are denied credit or employment, contacted by the police, or have to deal with collection agencies, credit cards, and bills.

A study on the aftermath of an identity theft by the nonprofit Identity Theft Resource Center found that victims spend 600 hours recovering from the crime because they must contact and work with credit cards, banks, credit bureaus, and law enforcement. The time can add up to as much as $16,000 in lost wages or income.

The number of reported cases of identity theft is increasing steadily. There is no one reason for this, but rather this is due to several ways in which our lives have changed in recent years, all of which make it easier for people to obtain our personal information.

In the United States, Social Security numbers are used more commonly as a means of identification. The Internet has made the transmission of personal information easy and, at times, less secure. Online retailers store our credit card information and contact information in databases we assume to be secure.

Marketing databases not only contain personal information, but they aggregate information on our spending habits as well as contact information. But potentially nefarious employees of these companies could have access to that information. They can then sell it online in chat rooms where criminals meet to swap information.

Even in the days of e-mail and instant messaging, the postal mail can also play a surprising role in identity theft. Checks can be stolen from the outgoing mail.

Credit card companies bombard their customers and potential customers with pre- approved offers that need very little personal information to complete.

Credit card issuers also send what they call "courtesy checks" to customers who can use them to make charges on a card. Many experts consider them an invitation to identity theft.

One of the increasingly common ways that criminals try to obtain personal information is by using what is called a "phishing attack." If you have e-mail, the chances are good someone has tried to get you to bite.

Phishing combines a criminal attempt at obtaining personal information with another plague of the Internet age — spam. Potential victims receive an e-mail from what appears to a bank, an online payment company like PayPal, or a retailer like eBay or Amazon.com. The message is usually sent using HTML e-mail and, when opened, uses company logos and symbols to make it appear to be legitimate.

The e-mail asks the receiver for usernames, passwords, account numbers, or some other type of personal information by saying they are updating records or something related to their account requires their attention. The e-mail usually links to a site that also appears to be legitimate using logos and other symbols of a real company, where visitors are asked to supply the information.

The first step to avoid becoming the victim of a phishing attack is to know what companies do business with you by e-mail and familiarizing yourself with the types information they request and how they request it.

What you will likely learn quickly is that, while online retailers you frequent and financial services firms you use online often send you e-mail to make you aware of new products or services, or even to alert you when your online bill is ready to be viewed, they rarely if ever ask for any information from you.

Banks and financial services firms will never ask you for any personal information via e-mail because e-mail can be notoriously insecure. So any e-mail asking you for personal or account information, such as passwords, Social Security numbers, PINs, credit or check card numbers, or other confidential information should be deemed suspicious.

Often the sender of a phishing e-mail may appear to be legitimate, but e-mail addresses are easily spoofed. Just look at the amount of spam you probably get that appears to be from friends, co-workers, or even yourself.

If a phishing e-mail directs you to a link using an HTML e-mail, the text of the link may appear to be legitimate, but following that link often brings you to a Web site where the URL (in your Web browser's location bar) is often an IP address (basically, numbers separated by periods, like 128.0.0) or a site other than the institution you think sent you the e-mail.

Often a sense of urgency is conveyed in the e-mail, such as an alert saying your account will be closed if you don't provide information. Take a moment and don't fall for this.

A close look at the body of the e-mail itself may reveal typos, misspellings, or horrendously poor grammar. One reason for this is that many phishing attacks are launched from overseas, and many are believed to be related to international organized crime.

Despite all the attention phishing has received of late, there remains precious little enforcement of the widespread problem and there are simply too many attacks to handle. It is an easy buck for online criminals.

We already covered many of the ways you can detect a phishing attack, but there are several simple steps you can take to keep your private information safe that bear discussion. Experts say that educating consumers not to follow links in e-mails is a good way to help them avoid phishing attacks. Rather than following a link in an e-mail, open a browser and go to the site of the retailer or bank in question.

When submitting personal information like credit card numbers, you can ensure you are using a secure connection by looking for "https://" in front of the site's location on your browser rather than "http://."

Speaking of your browser, make sure it is up to date with the latest security patches. If you use Microsoft's Internet Explorer, visit WindowsUpdate.com to see if you need any updates.

Here are some simple software tools you can use to help guard against online identity theft:

> • CoreStreet makes a free product called SpoofStick for both the Internet Explorer and FireFox Web browsers that helps users avoid spoofed Web sites. If you do follow a link in a suspicious e-mail, SpoofStick can tell you if the Web site you visit really is the Web site you think you are visiting.

- The EarthLink toolbar which is also free to internet users, has a feature called ScamBlocker. EarthLink keeps a database of known phishers, and if you visit a page known to be operated by a phisher it will alert you right in your browser.

Unfortunately, correcting your credit report when you have become a victim of identity theft is no easy proposition. But with some patience and a lot of work, you can recover from identity theft and restore your credit report.

Identity theft can result in damage to your credit rating - damage that could take years to fix. Generally, victims of credit and banking fraud are liable for no more than the first $50 of the loss. In many cases, the victim will not be required to pay any part of the loss.

To reduce your risk of identity theft, protect personal information and do not carry your Social Security card with you. Shred items that contain your personal information and account numbers. Keep your mail safe and store your personal information in a safe place. Order your credit report at least once a year to make sure no one is using your identity to open accounts.

If you think your identity has been stolen, take the following steps:

- Contact the three major credit bureaus. Contact the fraud departments of all of the three major credit departments to place a fraud alert on your credit file. The initial fraud alert is for 90 days. You can ask for an extended fraud alert if you file a police report.

• Close accounts. Close the accounts that you know or believe have been tampered with or opened fraudulently.

• File a police report. Get a copy of the report to submit to your creditors and others who require proof of the crime.

• File your complaint with the Federal Trade Commission (FTC) The FTC maintains a database of identity theft cases, which is used by law enforcement agencies for investigations. Filing a complaint also helps us learn more about identity theft and the problems it causes victims.

• Armed with your police report, FTC affidavit, and sample letters, you must contact your creditors to alert them to the situation. In addition to obvious creditors like your credit card issuers, don't forget utility companies, wireless phone provider, and your ISP.

Also remember any private label credit cards to department stores, for example. Don't forget about other personal documents. If your passport was stolen, for example, or if you have reason to believe someone is using a passport in your name, contact the State Department.

When you are trying to correct your credit report due to identity theft, you will have to provide information that proves you are you. That means digging out your birth certificate and making a lot of copies of your driver's license and social security card. You'll also have to try and prove that you didn't make the purchases that the thief or thieves did.

When you have become a victim of identity theft through phishing, this becomes a real problem as these purchases can be made anywhere with a few strokes of the keyboard, so proving that the purchases were made by someone other than you can be a real headache.

Just try to be patient and point out to the company or companies who say you owe them money that you have filed a police report as well as a report with the FTC and that you have been a victim in other places as well.

As we've said, it will take time, but it can be done. Your credit rating and credit score is very important, so taking the time to do will pay off in the long run. Realize that in the long run, you'll be able to enjoy good credit again.

Even if you are denied credit, you can appeal the decision by pointing out that you have been a victim of identity theft and are trying to correct it.

Now let's take a look at ways you can raise your present credit score.

Jeni Temen

Raising Your Credit Score

Let's say you want to buy a house but your credit score is somewhere around 675 instead of 720 which will get you the best rate on a home loan. If you want to raise your credit score quickly, there are some steps you can take that can guarantee a great home loan or any other credit line for that matter.

The mantra for getting a great score is pay your bills on time, keep account balances low, and take out new credit only when you need it. People who do that faithfully have very high scores. It usually means you're being conservative and cautious about credit. It's not a toy and it shouldn't be a hobby.
That's good advice, to be sure, but these actions take a long time. What if you're house hunting and you just need a few extra points to bump you over the line to the great rates? As we've said before, the first place to start is with your credit report. Check it over and find out what your credit score is right now.

You will want to concentrate mostly on correcting any errors by taking the steps we've outlined above. Look for errors such as accounts that aren't yours, late payments that were actually paid on time, debts you paid off that are shown as outstanding, or old debts that shouldn't be reported any longer.

Negatives are supposed to be deleted after seven years, with the exception of bankruptcies, which can stay for as long as 10 years.

After repairing errors, the fastest route to a better score is paying down balances on credit cards. There's really no silver bullet, but over 60 days' time it is possible to increase your score 20 points by paying down your credit lines.

Had a few late payments in your past? If you find yourself in some financial difficulties, you can protect your score by making sure your payments don't go 60 days past due. Some lenders don't report 30 days past due, but they all report 60 days past due.

Even if you've paid your bills late in the past, you can improve your credit score by paying every bill on time from now on. Forget about grace periods. If you want to have a really good record with the credit agencies, pay your debt before it's due and keep your balances low.

One thing you shouldn't do if you're just trying to boost your score is close unused accounts. If someone tells you to close unused accounts to improve your score, they're pulling your leg. It won't help you and it can actually hurt you.

Closing unused accounts without paying down your debt changes your utilization ratio, which is the amount of your total debt divided by your total available credit. You appear closer to maxing out your accounts. That's why your score can drop. It doesn't mean people shouldn't close them, but don't close them to improve your score.

If you do cut up cards, though, leave the oldest one open. The length of your credit history is another factor in your score. If you close the account of the credit card you got when you were a freshman in college and leave open the ones you just got within the last couple years, it makes you look like a much newer borrower.

Another strategy for bringing up your score is to transfer balances from a card that's close to being maxed out to other cards to even out your usage. You can also just spread out your charges between a few cards. Try to get the usage on all of them at 20 to 30 percent instead of a bunch at zero and one at 80 percent. You're not spending less; you're just shifting it around to different cards. Transferring the balance to a card with a lower utilization could help, but it's much better to actually pay down the debt if you have the cash kicking around.

If you're really into finessing the system, check your credit report to see what day of the month your creditors send updates on payments to the credit bureaus. They're rarely on the same cycle as your payment due date. That's why you can pay off your card every month and your credit report will show you carrying a balance. Then, make your payments several days before the reporting date.

All of these strategies generally take at least 30 days because lenders don't report payments more than once a month.

If you're in the throes of qualifying for a mortgage and need a score boost in a hurry, you can speed the process along with rapid rescoring. If you've got legitimate negative information on your credit report, such as late payments or accounts in collections, you're out of luck. But the process of rapid rescoring can help increase your score within a few days by correcting errors or paying off account balances.

You can't do this one yourself; you'll need a lender who is a customer of a rapid rescoring service. Generally, the service will run roughly $50 for every account on your credit report that needs to be addressed, but it could save you thousands on your loan. If a consumer can find a lender who is a customer of a rapid rescoring service, new information can be posted within 72 hours.

There's a lot of information that we've presented to you in previous section, So, let's do a little recap on the more important points.

To review

The very first thing that you must do in order to raise your credit score is to order your free annual credit report and find out what your credit score is. Once you have obtained copies of your credit reports from all three-credit reporting agencies: Experian, Equifax, and TransUnion, you must take the time to go over those reports to check for errors and inconsistencies.

It is imperative that you correct any mistakes or inconsistencies as soon as possible. This is the most pro-active step you can take for yourself to increase your credit score as mistakes can and do happen. Look for accounts that were previously delinquent but which have since been paid off. Find any accounts that were closed or any accounts that aren't yours. Then take steps to correct those errors by contacting the credit bureaus and beginning the process in writing to have these errors removed from the report. This alone can raise your credit score.

Checking your credit report often can also indicate if you have become a victim of identity theft which is something that is happening over and over again with frightening frequency. It affects millions of people and can wreak havoc with your credit rating.

Correcting the problem of identity theft is a process that will take quite some time, but it can be done with patience and excellent documentation. You should definitely be contacting the FTC and filing a police report in this situation so that you credibility cannot be called into question.

In the above section, we discussed extensively the option of filing for bankruptcy. This should be done only as a last resort and if you are in dire financial straits that cannot be solved if you just don't have the means to pay off your debts.

Filing for bankruptcy doesn't have the stigma attached to it that it once did and is nothing to be ashamed of. While it's true that the bankruptcy will remain on your credit report for up to ten years, lenders know that you will not be able to file for bankruptcy again within that time frame, so you may actually be able to obtain credit anyway after a bankruptcy.

Before you resort to a bankruptcy filing, you can first try getting the advice of a credit counselor to help get you back on track when it comes to your money problems. Find a reputable company that provides results and know that you will be paying a small fee for this service, but one that will probably be worth it in the end.

Credit counseling companies not only work with your creditors to secure lower repayment rates, but they provide financial planning advice for you to use in the future so you are not put in the same situation you were in before.

If you do have steady income, you may want to look into a debt consolidation loan. That way you can pay off your creditors and make one monthly payment to one company instead of several monthly payments to several companies.

There are also companies who can help with debt consolidation loans although you can certainly do it on your own. They can, however, secure loans for you with a lower interest rate and shop around to different companies to find you the best debt consolidation loan and help you get out of debt.

If you have bad credit, expect to take about a year or two to get it up to a letter credit rating. How do you do this? Let's review:

- Pay your bills on time. This alone will show good faith to your creditors and have a positive effect on your credit rating

- Don't use credit at all if possible. That means cutting up your credit cards and paying cash for the things you need.

- You may want to keep one credit card that you can use for emergencies – but remember that it is for emergencies only. Keep the oldest card you have as that shows you are not newly applying for credit.

• A good idea for not using that one credit card is to freeze it in a block of ice. It won't damage the card and it will require thawing before you can use it. That way, you will have to wait before making a purchase thus eliminating the lure of an impulse purchase.

• Don't apply for new lines of credit at all. The only time you should ever be applying for credit when you are financial straits is if you need to make a big purchase such as a vehicle or home.

• Monitor your credit report faithfully and immediately correct any mistakes that you find.

• If you find that you cannot make a payment on time, call your creditor and explain the circumstances. If you have been a good customer, they may be willing to accept a late payment and waive the late fees. Try not to do this too often as it can reflect poorly on your payment history.

• If you have little to no credit, you can establish credit by obtaining a department store or gas credit card. Then you make a few purchases and pay the balance off immediately.

• Be very careful when making purchases online. Make sure that when you are entering in your credit card number it is done on a web site that starts with https://. The "s" at the end of the http designation shows that it is a secure sight that will keep your information private.

• Beware of "phishing" e-mails that direct you to a separate site where you are asked to provide personal information. This is how many identity thieves obtain your bank account or credit card numbers and they can run up horrendous bills in a few moments of time.

• If you want to obtain a large loan as for a vehicle, you may want to try and get a co-signer who has good credit. Their good name and credit history can help you get the loan and build your credit at the same time. Be aware that co-signer will be liable for that loan like it is his/her. You should not default or pay late! If you do that, you will ruin their credit as well as yours. Being responsible will benefit you and the co-signer.

• Again, we want to iterate the most important thing about maintaining good credit and raising your credit score: **MAKE YOUR PAYMENTS ON TIME!** And use credit sparingly.

There are a lot of great tools available online to help you with credit and making credit decisions. Go to www.myfico.com and check out some of their calculators. Since FICO is the company who assigns you that magic little number that is your credit score, they are a great source of help for the consumer.

At this site, you can find out:

- Which loan is better
- How much your mortgage payments will be
- How much money you can afford to borrow
- Whether or not you are better off refinancing a loan
- How much refinancing costs will be
- Whether or not you should consolidate your credit cards
- How long it will take to pay off a credit card balance
- How rate changes will affect your loan balance
- And much, much more!

You can also find many other websites that can help guide you through not only the credit process but how to get and maintain a solid credit score and rating.

Last, but not least, don't forget the three major credit card reporting agencies. These are the places you should start to obtain your credit report and get on your way toward better credit.

- Experian: www.experian.com
- TransUnion: www.transunion.com
- Equifax: www.equifax.com

Plus, you can also go to the following websites to obtain your annual free credit report that is available once a year to all consumers:

- www.annualcreditreport.com
- www.freecreditreport.com

Jeni Temen

Conclusion

You can repair your own credit, just like an attorney or a credit repair agency would. You just need to negotiate yourself with individual creditor. Never be afraid or intimidated, they are there to collect. Debt collectors are considered successful if they collect anything, any amount be 1cent on a dollar.

They **WANT** to negotiate with you even if they act like they don't. It helps to have cash available to negotiate a debt item. You need to be prepared to pay right than when they agree, but make sure you're talking to a legitimate person and not a scammer. Also make sure you get a note or negotiation ID number to prove if needed.

Keep accurate and precise notes, who you talked to, what day and time and exactly what were you promised. You might need to send that to the credit reporting agency. Always, always check your credit a few weeks after you negotiated to make sure it reflects the arrangement you made.

Below are some forms you can use to negotiate.

Like I said at the beginning of this book, we are a country in debt. One person I know once told me that it was "The American Way" to buy things on credit and then owe people money. While that might not be the best way to think about it, when the price of things like vehicles and homes is well beyond what we would be able to pay cash for, we have to face the reality that credit is necessary.

In all actuality, the concept of credit has actually been around for a very long time. Anyone who is a fan of "Little House on the Prairie" knows that when the Ingalls would go to the General Store, they would always put their items "on account" which would be paid later – usually when the crops were in or Paw got paid from his various jobs.

Back then, credit reports and credit scores weren't necessary. It was an unwritten rule that the accounts would eventually be paid. A man's word was his name and their name meant everything back then. Collection agencies weren't necessary and accounts always got paid even if took some time. The shop owners didn't worry and were willing to wait. It was the law of the settlers albeit and unwritten one!

Then we continued to want more and more in our lives and "stuff" became almost necessary in our minds. As time passed, accounts weren't being paid and businesses were asked to take hits from people who reneged on their agreements.

This brings us to where we are today: a nation in debt. Even the Federal Government is in debt. It only goes to follow that citizens would be in debt too.

That said, we know we need credit to obtain the things we need – and often those that we don't. Credit card companies are preying on people at a younger and younger age. That puts young people alarmingly in debt before they even get to the legal drinking age.

That's why it's so important to know about credit and when it should be used as well as when it shouldn't be used. Practice smart credit procedures and don't overextend yourself. You can easily find yourself in trouble before you even know it. Then the time comes to change your spending habits, make smart credit decisions and take steps to raise your credit score. No matter what situation you might find yourself in regarding your credit, you can not only get out of debt, but you can restore your credit and enjoy a high credit score.

It takes time and a little bit of effort, but it certainly can be done. You just need to be diligent about your spending habits and then monitor your credit reports so you know where you stand at any particular time.

Credit is an important part of our society, so cherish your credit history and your credit score. Make it just as important to you as your good name and keep it clean and pristine. It can mean so much to your future and your future is just as important as the present.

You know what they say: The past is the past, the future is the future, but today is a gift – that's why they call it the present!

Good Luck!

The following websites were referenced in researching this book:

www.moneycentral.com
www.myfico.com
www.about.com
www.experian.com

Your Family Budget

Jeni Temen

Family Budgets
A Brief Introduction

"The average family exists only on paper and it average budget is a fiction, invented by statisticians for the convenience of statisticians."

-Sylvia Porter

Unlike the quote provided above, seemingly reflective of general opinion on family budgets today, we will attempt to take a much more positive approach to budgeting, as a family oriented, user-friendly, financial management and planning tool and life-enabler.

However, when reflecting on family budgeting and inquiring as to why not more families are actually, using it, it becomes self-evident that similar skepticism runs rampant and deep in reality and society, even globally so.

Once you start probing family budgets, expending time and energy researching the subject in- depth, it becomes quite clear, that most families are caught in a vicious, almost never-ending cycle of *"What comes in must go out."*

Most families might feel that budgeting is a futile effort, unnecessarily burdening them with thoughts and ways, to go broke methodically and slowly, without the creature comforts and indulgences of our human modern-day society.

Others might voice that they feel as if they are merely throwing money away, in a never-ending and dizzying spiral of spend, spend, spend. People are getting deeper and deeper into debt, no matter how hard they try to get out of it.

Questions are then raised:

How do we stop these courses of action?

How do we change the thinking around family fiscal discipline?

Put simply, in "How to set up a Family Budget", we focus in on how to empower families to set up better, more realistic budgets, stick to them and celebrate their successes (and learn from failures!)

Families eventually will have a monthly surplus, see their savings start to grow, consolidate their debt, set aside discretionary funds and personal allowances, build their wealth and become more aware of their pro-active involvement and responsibility regarding their lives and finances. This is when excitement builds up, fundamental thought patters and spending attitudes are changed.

Budgeting is seen as an accurate measurement of success when significant behavioral is taking place on the landscape of the family budget, spending habits and financial patterns we observe over time!

Do you ever feel that you do not have enough cash at the end of the month to pay bills, buy necessities of life? Are you barely making a dent in your credit card debt balance, no matter how hard you try?

Here is a reality check for all of us: if we choose to spend it, it is gone for good. We can't spend it on anything else. Are you perhaps worried about a nest egg for your golden years or savings for early retirement? Then you have arrived at a source that can provide some prudent tips on how to start, finish, implement, stick to, revise and refine a family budget.

The family budget is a dynamic process, even more so than a mere static work-product, result, process-outcome or document. It will, can and should change over time. It becomes a barometer of a family's fiscal circumstance, resources and health.

Maybe budgeting is not as much about reflecting on what you cannot have, but more about thoughts on how to stretch, invest and spend your earned dollars more wisely. In short, it is about making your money going further.

This quick-reference how-to guide was developed to assist you with setting up your own personal, household and family budget, to help you with all of the above and more!

A couple of general money-savings will also be provided in these pages. There are also thoughts and spending patterns that need to change, in order to become fiscally more disciplined and any techniques, attitudes, habitual behaviors that we need to unearth, evaluate and possibly change, before you even start budgeting.

For example, being a bargain hunter looking for good buys, cutting down on careless spending, being on the lookout for careless credit card spending and letting the person who handles money best in your household actually take care of it, are all good examples of what we mean.

For most households, a budget is no more than a spending plan. Any spending plan can help you see where your money is going. It fits your spending to your income. It reflects how we get the things we want and need most, while being ready and prepared for bills we must pay every month.

For most families it is simply about making a budget you can live with and stick to easily. It's not a difficult exercise, but one most people fear, avoid or dread because of the unknown and perceived complexity of it (sometimes wrongfully so!).

Part of the goal of this guide is to demystify family budgeting and highlight an easy systematic process to setting up a quality family budget. Many things actually drive our expenditure. We choose to spend our money on things we value, need, prefer or consciously choose. For some it is clothes, for others it might be something as simple as taking that yearly vacation.

Whether you are making financial decisions for yourself or your household, you might have to make some serious choices and adjustments regarding your financial freedom and situation.

This is a quick-reference, easy, how-to guide, meant to take you through the typical, who, why, when, what, where and how questions typically asked when considering fiscal planning for the household and or budgeting in general for your family need, means and circumstance, now and for the future.

Budgeting is not just about restricting spending and living a cheapskate life. It is about insights, wisdom, informed decisions, action and sustained discipline when it comes to your household financials.

This guide will invite you to learn more in these pages about systematic budgeting. It focuses on practical application and zooms in to apply these "best practice suggestions" in your own home. It empowers you to put together a dynamic, financial plan that suits your pocketbook, means and circumstance.

- Financially speaking, assess quickly where you think you and your family are today.
- What kind of a picture do you have?
- Could you come up with something?
- Did you have the data and numbers you needed?
- Would you be able to plan for where you want to be and start living your life today as a fiscally sound and disciplined family with the information you have at your disposal at present?

Money makes the world go round! It is no secret that some of us have more, some have less. We deal with our own personal finances and cash management distinctly differently. Households have varying needs, means and circumstance. Our money-management skills are also, at different levels, as is our debt and savings!

Budgeting has to do with most of these perspectives and reflections.

The purpose and goal of family budgeting is:

(i) financial situational analysis and informed awareness,

(ii) cutting cost,

(iii) gaining control or curbing spending and

(iv) Starting to save, building up wealth and liquid assets over time.

There are many phases and steps to go through when creating a budget.

If you are looking for ways to manage your money better, making it reach and stretch further, and providing you with financial security and a more solid future, then you have come to the right place In this brief introduction on family budgets, we have already introduced our first couple of key questions:

Why a book or how-to guide on setting up a family budget?

Why do you need a family budget?

What is the business case for and rationale behind family budgeting?

What are the benefits and advantages of a family budget?

Why a Book on Setting Up a Family Budget?

We elaborate a little more below. For most people, a family budget is the equivalent of a simplistic process: **money is earned and comes in; money is spent and moves out!**

It is a fluid, easy-flow, one-directional, cash management process. It is driven by daily life, a spending-orientation, or no plan at all! For most families, income is also fixed and outflow typically increases over time, as the needs of the family fluctuates and changes. Loading up on debt is also very typical for the majority of our families. If this sounds very much like a vicious circle, it is. Most families are caught up in it and constantly battle to get out.

Mostly, we think that we wisely spend our money on necessities like food and clothing, gas and household or family needs, but can rarely put a finger on where the money actually goes, let alone produce a budget!

A good place to start is to monitor these expenses.

Take stock of your fiscal situation. Start with assessing where exactly you are in your financial life and circumstance. Most of us think we know, but we really do not. That is, until we take the time to actually list, study and analyze the situation. Figure out what your financial worth is, look at all financial goals, and set a timeline for reaching them. Does this sound like an action plan? Where do you start?

A good suggestion is your bank statements, tax return and recent current credit report – a financial asset statement if you will -and an overview of the current situation.

The premise is simple: you can not get to arrive where you want to be if you do not know where you are today, what it will take to get where you need to be and how to get there.

A well thought out, planned and realistic budget will serve as a roadmap to get you there. It is a financial tool facilitating your financial dreams, goals and aspirations, making them become a reality. Budgeting will enable you to actually reach your financial targets and set goals.

Do You Need a Family Budget?

How do you define financial worth? Is it cash in the bank, savings and checking accounts, RRSP's, stocks and investment portfolio?

Remember, anything you have that is of value counts. All your assets form part of your financial picture and health. Ask yourself: What is your take-home pay, after deductions? How are you paid? Is it monthly, weekly, bi-weekly? Then you need to budget accordingly!

Think about all other sources of income, temporary, seasonal, part-time - extra income, found money and bonuses that you might have.

Maybe deciding to leave it out of your family budget altogether is wise and advisable? (we will delve into this question a little later).

Try to find ways to do without some small creature comforts and pleasures to reap bigger rewards later.

Starting small, early and now, with discipline and commitment, a steady, consistent pace and amount every month, tracking and optimizing financial phenomena like 'compound interest' (which we will describe later), will all feed into this process.

We will take this journey into budgeting together to see how it can change lives: yesterday, today and tomorrow!

Back to listing assets and thinking about savings: consider all banks, savings and loans, credit union accounts, money market accounts, certificates of deposit, Christmas club accounts you might have. ALL LIQUID ASSETS that can be readily turned into cash need to be included.

Consolidate accounts if you have too many accounts spread out and save on banking fees.

Improve tracking actual spending better and more easily. Earn higher interest and have less exposure to identity theft or fraud by getting a good handle on your current situation.

For most individuals and families alike, this step is quite a revelation. It forms the basis and baseline for deeper analysis and scrutiny.

Other assets might include things like: art, precious metals, sculptures, paintings, collections, antiques, jewelry and more.

Most of us are used to having a short-term focus on money and budgeting. A paradigm-shift is required to move us towards a more in-depth, longer-range view and planning.

Set short, mid and long term goals, have a definite structured plan, read up on family budgeting, personal financials and fiscal management strategies. All of this will help us focus on what is important for our needs, requirements and circumstance, while keeping financial discipline and budgeting in the forefront of our busy lives.

This is never an easy task amidst all the hustle and bustle that is our daily lives!

Most of the published literature on family budgeting in general centers around how to get out of debt, stay out of debt and live a full and prosperous life.

Some suggest frugal living is the answer, and offer 'your money or your life' perspectives, where you can't have both. There are many examples advocating the cheapskate monthly makeover that focuses on shaving costs off expenses and living frugally.

Market providers both online and offline, offer various budget kits which offers worksheets and more and there is always the handy tip-like Coles notes and the pocket idiots' guide to living on a budget.

Other sources focus on becoming totally debt free, debt proofing your life, getting a life and choosing simplicity or how to address credit card debt and expenditure.

This 'how to' guide is a little different.

We have chosen to take a very hands-on, practical approach to fiscal management and get you started, walking through the budgeting steps and set you up, sending you off, well and good, on- course to solid budgeting in your family and household!

This brings us to the Who, What, When, Where, Why and How part of the discussion. These form the dynamic, interacting and inter-dependent elements, systems and processes that form a family, or household budget.

Who?
- Every family situation is uniquely different and distinctive. There is no one-size-fits-all answer and solution for everyone.

Some of the tips in this guide might apply to your unique means and circumstance, and others may not have any significant impact or practical application at all.

In general terms, you will find handy ideas, hints, process steps, practical savings suggestions and budgeting that might have gone unnoticed before.

The information provided is general and should be evaluated on an individual and contextualized basis. Remember to consult a financial advisor when making fiscal decisions that could affect the financial health, well-being and future of you and your treasured family.

There are various different families in question here too: single-income, single-parent, blended and/or extended families, double-income households, stay-at-home mothers working part-time from home to make ends meet, social-supported and/or subsidized families, families at risk, divorced household with shared parenting and financial responsibilities, debt-ridden or bankruptcy families and numerous others. We hope to offer something for everyone.

What?
- Family budgeting is a structured process and planning activity, dealing with a family's financial resources and context.

This hands-on approach puts expense items into categories as another helpful strategy. This is done to get a better handle on the current situation and offers somewhat of a reality check to most that choose to undertake this journey.

Some of the categories could be:

- Obligations – list each item under headings like: home: mortgage or rent; association fees and professional dues; insurance: health, auto, home, renters' and life; tuition, day care; loans: car loan, student loan, bank fees and interest; taxes, property taxes and so on.

- Necessities – again list each item under headings like : food, groceries, gas, yard maintenance, security, pest control, utilities: gas, water, electric, garbage, sewer; school lunches, household supplies, car maintenance, monthly parking, housekeeper, household repairs, internet service, dry cleaning, cable TV and more.

- Pocket expenses – treat this as a whole category, covering: lunch at work, snacks, sodas, coffee, drinks, parking, tolls, newspapers, magazines, batteries, postage, shipping, mail

- Family Allowances – another whole category including items like : parties, entertainment, weekend outing, movies, concerts, other entertainment and events, home improvements and decorating, magazine and other subscriptions, dining out and fast food, furniture

- Personal allowances - clothing, hobbies, personal recreation, books, manicures, hair, alterations, shoe repair, personal gifts, luggage, night out with friends, gardening, films, processing, video rentals, sports / recreation, family gifts, contributions, donations, computer software and other related items.

When and Where?

In the interest of brevity, we combine the next two facets. Our best assessment to answering when and where the best place and time would be to start a family budget would be to answer unequivocally: **HERE AND NOW!**

It demands attention as it directly affects our daily lives and well-being. Without delay, hesitation or postponement, we need to step up and protect our family interest, financial health and future.

Accounting brings accountability! A wealth management guru is often quoted as saying. This rings so true. It is hard to ignore, if we are confronted with objective cold hard financial facts that tell us that we are in trouble.

Why budget?

Families, as mentioned before, have diverse reasons and motivations for budgeting. Briefly summarized, people budget for a couple of reasons:

- To gain control of their financial life, monthly bills and spending

- Be prepared and avoid surprises

- Save for a major purchase

- Opt out of a vicious circle of ever-spiraling debt or spend-now-pay-later thinking

- Expand their lifestyle(s)

- Retire early

- Eliminate money as a source of tension and topic for argument

- Rediscover that the best things in life are FREE!

- Becoming self-reliant and empowered to know that debt does not rule their lives anymore!

I promise even more on this a little later!

Benefits and Advantages of a Family Budget

How to budget? Some general strategies are helpful in assisting families to set up a budget or budget better.

1) The first significant step is to change your thinking about money, shift your attitude toward spending, focus on saving money, plan ahead and drive for success.

2) Develop a greater awareness of how you earn, manage, save and spend money

3) Awareness of how others would lure, entice and want you to spend your money (advertisers, retailers, and manufacturers)

4) To stop participating and playing the "Keeping-up-with-the-Jones's game," living with a false sense of wealth and security, while over-extending yourself and financial resources, beyond your means. Do not envy others and lust after things that they might have or even worse, get deeper into debt to compete or keep up appearances. It is counterproductive and can ruin lives!

5) Delay purchases – learn and do, sometimes without having to buy!

6) Set solid financial and budget goals for yourself and your family that you can do individually and collectively to achieve together

- Set spending limits and stick to them

- Do not make ends meet utilizing credit cards, stay away from ATM machines, cash, cash advances, do not cheat on your budget

- Understand your income – know where the money is coming from and how it varies throughout a one-year cycle

- Understand your expenses – monthly and irregular, unexpected expenses

- Set a few realistic financial goals

- Know your own habits, spending, temptation, and where the areas of risk and exposure are.

- Set up savings and spending mechanisms that work, reserve and growth accounts and have the right number of credit cards

- Make an income plan – detail is important

- Plan your obligations and must pays – smooth out large size bills with reserve accounts

- Plan your necessities and look for ways to economize

- Set aside pocket money for daily incidentals

- Create a family allowance to cover entertainment

- Create a personal allowance

- Balance and consolidate, wise decisions and trade-offs – agree and stick to it

- Live happily on a budget

- Welcome to frugal living mode! Cutting back on living expenses – alternatives for simple living

- Re-examine why you work and how you live

- Stop tossing your hard-earned cash away

- Shopping, overwork, stress and debt (some refer to this as an illness quipped: 'Affluenza'!)

- Celebrate when you have money left over at the end of the month – indulge a little and reward yourself – rewarding patience and persistence! Not just the doing good and sticking with it

The Rationale and Process of Budgeting

Family budgets are used as a baseline, analysis-tool and roadmap. It is a useful tool and guide. It tells you whether you are headed in the direction you want to be headed in financially. It helps you to move from spending to saving and good fiscal balance, management and responsibility.

Here are twelve plus good reasons to get you started:

- You may have goals and dreams, but if you do not set up guidelines for reaching them and you do not measure your progress, you may end up going so far in the wrong direction you can never make it back. Can you imagine the government or a major corporation operating without a budget? No, and neither should you.

- It is often described and justified as an empowering enabler. A budget lets you control your money instead of your money controlling you.

- A budget is a realistic estimate and true reflection of current circumstance and means, a type of financial situation-analysis that will tell you if you are living within your means.

Before the widespread use of credit cards, you could tell if you were living within your means because you had money left over after paying all your bills.

There are lots of family budgeting tools available online that make it a fun and enjoyable task and activity, to assess and analyze your family's financial situation with minimum effort.

www.MoneyPants.com

There is also lots of free financial software and most of it sets up easily and provides you with a detailed family budget online. It manages your finances, hassle-free and almost effortless.

Well, almost! It will require input and minimum effort through hands-on involvement in setting it up, populating, maintaining and editing it.

www.Mvelopes.com is a good example of market offerings that are available at no cost to you, just waiting for the motivated family budgeter to embrace and try it out!

Some websites offer free financial newsletters by e-mail, with lots of money saving tips, budget advice, and other relevant personal and family-related financial information www.planabudget.com

The availability, accessibility, virtual marketplace, ease of use and more of credit cards has made the need for family budgets much less obvious. Many people do not even realize they are living far beyond their means until they are knee deep in debt, struggling to make ends meet and sinking fast into murky financial waters.

Budgeting is and can be a life and money saver, a reality check, **BUT ALSO** a remedy!

• A budget can help you meet your savings goals. It includes a mechanism for setting aside money for savings and investments.

• Following a realistic budget frees up spare cash so you can use your money on the things that really matter to you instead of frittering it away on things you do not even remember buying.

• A budget helps your entire family focus on common goals. It is unifying families in mutual purpose and effort, working together towards a successful outcome and reward.

• A budget helps you prepare for emergencies or large or unanticipated expenses that might otherwise knock you for a loop financially.

• A budget can improve your marriage. A good budget is not just a spending plan; it is a communication tool. Done right, a budget can bring the two of you closer together as you identify and work towards common goals and reduce arguments about money.

• A budget reveals areas where you are spending too much money, so you can refocus on your most important goals.

- A budget can keep you out of debt or help you get out of debt.

- A budget actually creates extra money for you to do use on things that matter to you.

- A budget helps you sleep better at night because you do not lie awake worrying about how you are going to make ends meet.

Nevertheless, despite all these wonderful reasons quoted above, people are still hesitant to commit to family budgeting as standard practice in their households. We might again want to probe a little deeper still and ask why?

Top Three Causes of Budget Failure

Many people make an honest attempt to budget, but become discouraged and give up before they are able to accomplish any significant financial gain. The top three causes of budget failure come into play before you even begin to set up your budget. Awareness of these budget busters, is your first line of defense in the Battle of the Budget.

Budget Buster #1 - Negative Attitude

It cannot be emphasized enough--a positive attitude about budgeting is essential to your success.

If you think of budgeting in negative terms (such as a financial diet, financial handcuffs, restrictive, penny-pinching, a sacrifice, etc.), you are sure to fail, unless you are a martyr or a masochist who finds some strange reward in a punishing experience. For purposes of this article, we will assume that you are neither.

A positive attitude means you think of a budget as a means to an end--a way to achieve your dreams and goals--and that postponing the instant gratification of spending all the money you earn is worth the rewards you will earn in the end.

Budget Buster #2 - Lack of Motivation

What is your motivation for budgeting? Are you trying to appease a nagging spouse? Following the terms of a debt repayment plan with a consumer credit counseling agency? Complying with an agreement made in bankruptcy court? These are not bad motivations, but they are external pressures and will probably not be easy to maintain over time. The best motivations are internally generated: do you honestly believe that budgeting can help you meet your goals?

If you need a little help in the motivation department, see the chapter "Twelve plus Reasons Budgeting Can Improve Your Life". A quick re-read of these will surely inspire and ignite a motivational spark or two!

Budget Buster # 3 - Unrealistic Expectations

What do you expect to gain from instituting and following a budget? Do you think that setting up a budget will reveal large caches of hidden cash or that the budget fairy will sprinkle fairy dust over your budget and magically transform your spending habits after a month or two of tracking expenses?

The reality is that budgeting is an endurance event--those who stick with it, through thick and thin, will come out ahead financially. Do not expect miracles. What you WILL see if you stick with it is steady, measurable progress towards the goals that really matter to you.

Starting a budget without having a positive attitude, internal motivation, and realistic expectations, will probably set you up for failure. You can greatly increase your chances of success by ruling out the three biggest budget busters before you even begin.

Family budgeting- just the thought of it makes most people cringe. However, mostly, we do attempt to curb spending and live within our own means. Others fall into bad habits, habitual spending patterns or impulse shopping and over-extend themselves, landing knee-deep in debt!

Ironically, one of the first remedies for any debt consolidation or repair strategy, is to take a long hard look at the budget and financial patterns within the household! It is almost like running a diagnostic.

To take a closer look, you are in effect placing your family dollars under a magnifying glass and microscope. This can prove both challenging and painful for most people. We hope to alleviate some of that initial discomfort and apprehension with this handy step-by-step guide and tips.

Most financial advisors will tell you that you have to reward yourself for good fiscal responsibility, discipline and habits, to increase your motivation and success levels.

Budgeting is the first step, sticking with and to it, a close second and the sometimes overlooked but ever-important reward, has to keep the motivation going! To repeat and continue to experience the benefit of the budgeting cycle and discipline could be an uphill battle, but there are calmer seas ahead.

Cash management, savings, planning for retirement, setting financial goals etc. active and hands- on, is becoming increasingly important for the survival and well-being of our families everywhere.

Be your own best expert with coming up with new ideas on how to save money, budget better and spend less! Your unique strategies stem from a deep understanding of your own situation, demands, and needs. Discover which tips and ideas work best for you. After all, fiscal management and finances are definitely not a one-size-fits-all solution environment. It is personal, customized and unique.

In the following section, we will briefly refer back to the family budget defined and look at some of its elements and criteria, purpose and functions such as:

What is a family budget?

What constitutes a good family budget?

What should it contain and look like?

Family Budgets Defined

What is the family budget? It is a pro-active, hands-on approach, focused, technical and disciplined strategy to getting a handle on the current financial situation in the home and family,

It concerns setting realistic, SMART financial goals for the household, sticking to it, celebrating successes, learning from failures and trying again if you do not succeed or get it right the first time round. It is about shifting focus completely from a mainly spending to a savings orientation.

Cash and money-management 101 for everyone!

We have laid out what a family budget is, does and affects. A brief mention of what constitutes as good family budget and the elements that it contains as well as its appearance, format and functional role follows.

All of us have a wish list of new things that we want. There is always things we would find and places to spend our money. Take the time to make a list of these things. Let everyone who shares cost in your home to have input into making and finalizing this list. Write down what you want most. Beside the goal, write how much it will cost. Split it into goals with ongoing costs and the cost per month, and goals with a one-time cost and list the actual total cost (including all hidden fees, taxes, shipping and or other charges that might apply. Now, next to these columns, start to prioritize these goals.

Which goal comes first?

You need to decide which goal on your list should cover with the other members of your family. If you live alone, think it over yourself. Try to list your top four goals and decide what you can fit into your budget.

A good budget is in the eyes of the creator or beholder alike! Some suggested but by no means comprehensive criteria follows:

- Budget is both process and product
- Collaborative, engaged, hands-on effort
- Characterized by communication and mutual agreement
- It advocates involvement and exchange
- It is real-time and reality-based
- Factual
- Accurate
- A financial check-up and check-in on the family finances, household dollars, situations, behaviors, and resources.
- An action-plan, future-oriented

- Offers a peak into the past, scrutinizes and enlightens the present, while planning and promising a future
- Goal and results oriented

How to Set Up a Good Family Budget

This brings us to the family budget process. We might ask questions like:

- How to set up a family budget?
- How should a family budget be used?

Insights around the tools and techniques of family budgeting could also be useful:

- Practical suggestions for setting up a budget?
- A step-by-step summary of a family budget process
- Hints, tips, tricks and tools for setting up a family budget

To get us started and in order to set up a monthly budget, follow these five easy steps:

Step one: find out your monthly take-home pay

Step two: find out what your expenses are

Step three: find out how much you spend on each expense

Step four: see if your monthly expenses match monthly take-home pay

Step five: balance your budget. This means in your family budget you need to ensure that you are spending matches take-home pay. It might indicate that you have to cut back on spending to balance.

It sounds too good to be true and too simplistic. However, in the end, that is all there is to this family budgeting process! Initially at least. Let us look at these steps one at a time.

Finding out your monthly take-home pay

Your income is your pay, after some money is deducted. Think taxes, insurance and Social Security. Answer the following questions:

- What is your monthly take home pay?
- Do other people share expenses in your home?

As mentioned before, total all of the households' monthly take-home pay. This will include all sources of income for all contributing members of the household.

Finding out what your expenses are

This brings up other pressing questions:

- Where does the money in fact go every month?
- What are your monthly expenses?

Most people are surprised to learn that it may go for things that we do not need at all. Writing your expenditures down provides us with the unique opportunity to visualize and find out if any money goes for things that we do not need or want.

Here is a short list of expenses that many people have. Put a check mark next to ones you have, then write down any expenses you have, that are not on the list.

- Necessities like food
- Clothes laundry dry-cleaning
- Car and transportation expenses: gas, oil, parking, license, plates, car repair, train fare or bus fare
- Rent, mortgage payments, heat, electricity, phone, water, property taxes, house repair, appliance and repair, furniture, small items for home, cleaning supplies on the yard care,
- Medical and dental expenses: doctor, dentist, drugs, hospital or clinic.
- Savings: short to medium term for something soon, a future purchase, emergencies, investments.
- Installment payments: car, furniture, appliances, charge accounts, credit card accounts, loans.
- Pocket money, personal allowances, tobacco, beer, wine and hair care.

- Entertainment, movies and eating out Recreation, sports and equipment, club membership,

newspaper, magazines, cable TV, records and tapes, DVDs videos and other multimedia, vacation, letters and postage.

- School bills, books, room and board at school, workshops, special training courses, lessons, music and more.

- Donations: church or synagogue, charitable giving, charities, other and gifts

- Insurance: (if not deducted from your paycheck): life, health, house, car and property

- Taxes: (if not deducted from your paycheck): Federal, state and local income, social security

Which other ones could you list?

- Finding out how much you actually spend on each expense

This is the hard part, where some thought and effort will have to go into the process to ensure the most accurate information is recorded. This will give a realistic and real-time estimate that is reliable and accurate.

In this section, you need to ask yourself how much each item on your list actually costs how much each item costs you a month.

The following estimates and guidelines could prove helpful to you as you set up your family budget:

- Monthly bills that stay the same - car and rental payments

- Monthly bills that change – utilities, phones and more. Find costs per month for say six months, add them up. Take this number you have calculated and divide it by six (the amount of months) to get your average cost.

This is the number you will be using for your budgetary exercise.

- Bills that come every three or six months– the number for every month will be used in your budgetary process.

- Bills that come annually – divide the amount by 12 months. The answer is your monthly budget number.

- Bills that come more than once a month – food, gas, lunch and family fun. This is a category to watch very closely, as it is a contributor to this "bottomless pit", we sometimes feel and see our cash disappear into.

- Unexpected expenses or surprise bills– what you can afford to set aside as a buffer or emergency, contingency fund - (look at the last three years or so and see what kind of unexpected expenses you and your family faced). Use an estimate that makes sense to you and divide the annual number by twelve months to get your monthly number.

• Finding out if monthly expenses match monthly take-home pay. Compare your total expenses with your take-home pay. A couple of results and scenarios could be staring you in the face:

Positive result: Income more than expense – you can either spend or save!

Negative result: Expense more than income – spending more than you have, you might have to cut costs and try to save some money to cover the bases!

Whichever of these outcomes you are faced with, knowing is better than not knowing.

For some this might bring little comfort and relief, but, people in general, find this exercise useful to make an unknown more measurable. It makes us accountable and wanting to act.

Finding ways to balance your budget

Earlier it was stated that a good budget would mean income would be equal to expenses. Having a small surplus is no guarantee by any means. You might need this to cover and unexpected rise in oil and gas prices or a larger grocery bill due to a party you are hosting at home.

This almost brings the concept home of a sliding scale, flexibility and discretionary buffer categories in budgets to absorb this give-and-take roller-coaster ride that is family budgeting.

The good news is whether you are in the red so to speak or just scraping by, managing to save nothing or maybe a little, or even a lot, this process will highlight areas where your attention is needed right away. It gives direction and purpose and assists families to formulate their spending plans, goals, re-visit their needs, dreams and goals.

Balancing the budget is no easy task. Here are a few steps that we can suggest to make your life a little easier:

- Find out how much you need to cut from your expenses

- Decide you can make cuts in your expenses and be detailed

- Re-balance your income and expenses after you've made these cuts

A word to the wise: Do not make cuts in your budget that you cannot live with in real life. It is extremely important to remain realistic and keep your real-time expenses and living realities in the forefront of your mind when you make these decisions.

If you're getting out of a situation where you are in debt and short of cash, you have to try to curb spending any way you can. Cutting those expenses are crucial, not only because you are over budget.

We mean that there might be other reasons, like adding a budget-line to your overall planning for your family vacation. Realistically, we cannot add and address new needs and goals before we have fulfilled our duty and responsibilities.

Cutting a little here and there will mostly do the trick – cancel that newspaper subscription for the papers that just land in the recycle box or garbage anyway. Do you need all the specialty channels and packages on your Cable TV options? Can you live with giving some up?

There is always the specter of rising prices and interest rates, inflation and more to cope with as well, so building preparedness for that into your budget is also a priority. Whatever we can do to cut our costs and expenditure will benefit our pocketbooks and family budgets immensely!

Cutting back on things you need the least is a good starting point if you are at a total loss as to what and how to give something up, add a new line into your budget or plan for the future or inevitabilities. You are well on your way in the family budgeting process. You are doing it, every step of the way. Consolidate and re-visit your budget often – it is a dynamic process and 'living' document or tools so to speak to help you keep your fingers on the pulse of your financial situation.

Another useful strategy is to set up a bill-paying plan and process that will protect your interest.

When how and how much you get paid will all influence your course of action. Creative and innovative allocation of your paycheck is the key.

If you get paid once a month, the amounts in your budget will have to be paid monthly as is.

If you get paid twice a month, divide each budget item by two.

If paid bi-weekly (as is mostly the practice these days), still divide the monthly amount by two – it will not be the exact amount to plan for, but a rough and close estimate. In the end better than nothing!

If you are paid weekly, divide each budget item into 4.

Cash flow management will form a big part of your fiscal strategy, once you have put your budget pen to paper and mapped out the needs and requirements. Utilize your cash, checking and savings account (if applicable) to pay for expenses. Do not pay your bills with your credit card!

Keep track of all your discretionary spending. A financial diary for a week is always a good idea to scribble down in every time you withdraw money, pay for something or open your purse without thinking.

This will provide you with insights you did not have before on where the money actually goes.

It will also carry within it, clues to adjust budget lines if actual cost is higher on certain items.

Spending patterns and behaviors will emerge that might surprise or shock you!

Having some wriggle-room and discretionary spending is always motivation. The occasional treat and indulgence, special night out or other family activity is that more enjoyable, if you know you have worked hard to earn it and deserve a pat on the back for all your fiscal responsibility and discipline!

Always keep one eye on the future folks… budgets might need to change again and again for a variety of reasons. You can never feel you have "arrived" completely and that your budget is set in stone. Family and life often throws us a curve ball or two, banks, service providers, government and fate sometimes do too!

Changing budgets should not be a source of frustration for you; it actually shows you that your family budgeting process is actually working. It is a real-time pulse and mechanism to capture these changes, which will leave you prepared and informed, ready to act and respond appropriately. This impetus for change can come from different sources.

Here are some examples:

Change of income, goals, rising prices, goals reached, family growing, moving and or relocating to a new place, family getting smaller, new spending habits, change in lifestyle or unplanned expenses.

If you can stick with it and see it through a family budget can help you meet your goals, get and stay out of debt, pay your bills on time, every time, keep track of your spending, cut costs and stretch your dollar to the max!

Jeni Temen

Hints, Tips, Tools and Tricks for Setting up a Family Budget

"Creating a budget" captures in its expression and meaning, both the excitement and the apprehension most of us feel when we have to face our financial situation and or lack of planning and accountability in that area.

Most businesses would fail if they ran like we manage our household incomes sometimes. This is to do. It falls into that 'I will if I really have no choice' kind of categories.

However, worth mentioning is that we spend most of our waking hours at work, earning the cash we need to get by and cover our living expenses. Then, we do not take the time to plan what to do with it. We just respond, spend and move on, spiraling, circling around, aimlessly and oblivious mostly about the state of our financial affairs.

This is obviously not true for some of us, for whom planning and organizing comes naturally and budgeting is like second nature and breathing, we just do not think about it, get it done and then barely spare it a second thought. Both these types of approaches can hurt us in the long run.

Our society has also become so fast-paced and focused on success, that we sometimes lose sight of the future perspective, enjoying life and what we do have. We cannot really focus on our own financials for lots of "excuses", sorry reasons we provide like: trouble slowing down, taking a step back and evaluating our financial situations or not knowing how to set up a family budget.

One of the first hints or tips we provide is advocating fiscal awareness. This means evaluating openly, freely and honestly where things are at today for your finances and household.

The whole purpose and goal of creating or setting up a family budget is to enlighten and alleviate money pressures. Utilizing a tool that can assist you in getting back onto the road to financial freedom, fiscal responsibility and financial, budgetary health, positive cash flow, with money to spare would be the ideal work-tool to grasp and grab! As the previous pages have shown the process in itself is not altogether that difficult.

You can certainly see how this real-time, 'dollar and expenditure tracker' can assist you to be agile and respond to market, family and monetary pressure, changes and crises. Continue to revise and update your budget as your needs, family and circumstances change.

Money is such a daily necessity and ever-present in our comings and goings. There is no escaping it. It is everywhere and needed anywhere and all over. We have different currencies, structures, procedures and all around the world, but in the end, it is the currency that makes the world go round, fueling the global economy.

Seen from that perspective, we often feel that taking control of our own finances and expenditures will not have much of an impact, as we are all at the mercy of the wheels and gear of a churning economical machine, with government and banking rules, regulations, trade and principles, ethics and decision-making that affects our quality of life. However, this is simply not the case!

Good money management skills in the household is crucial, not only for survival and good financial state of affairs, it teaches our children how we think handling money should be taken care of. They watch us so closely.

We model certain behaviors, spending patterns, discipline or maybe throwing all caution to the wind with credit card spending, debt and reminder notices all over the house, creditors calling, afraid to walk to the mailbox to remove the bills, and more.

What chance do our children have to end up entangled in that spiraling and vicious circle we spoke about earlier? Money in, money out?

How do we get to the point where family budgeting is a learning tool to help us teach our kids to work better with their funds? Whether through allowances, mutual savings goals, their own account or more, as parents we have an opportunity to instill some solid financial skills early on in life that will assist them later, as they work toward their independence and family budgets of their own!

Do some of your own soul-searching before you start your budgeting process. How motivated are you to plan, set-up and stick to a family budget? Would you do it now? Today? If you knew how?

Then let us get started, together. There are lots of practical suggestions for setting up a family or household budget. We will never be able to cover them or the mechanics and intricacies all here at once. You will however continue to find in these pages valuable insights and tit-bits to help you pursue better fiscal management and cash flow, budgeting in general.

It is all about making your dollar go further. Investing in the time and effort that it will take to get to that point of greater financial security and possibly even have a surplus eventually!

> - Take stock and face the facts head-on, honestly and with serious commitment, drive and purpose. Assessing your own capital worth and analyzing your home life and situation from a financial perspective is of utmost importance.
>
> - Plot your own course. Formulate some financial goals and lay out your own roadmap on how to

get where you need and want to be financially speaking.

• Take a thorough, critical and factual look at your fiscal situation and status. Unbiased and honest is best. Get a most recent credit report and look over your bank and credit cards statements, tax returns and other financial sources of information: stock portfolio, RRSP's and more.

• Get a financial planner to assist you if you are unsure about what to use and include or not in this assessment. You might also want to take a broader perspective and discuss retirement, priorities, insurance needs, will and testament and more, because, like financials, we never seem to take these crucial life planning tasks and to do very seriously and barely give them second thought or time of day! The time is now and the place is here to take control of your financial situation and life.

• Committing the time and effort to build your financial action and spending plan, budget and goals should get priority and might just be the most valuable undertaking and time well spent, not wasted you might ever set aside!

• Think of how you define your own financial worth. Reflect on what it is, what you base it on. Is it concrete data and fact, perception or maybe even a wild guess or estimate? Income, savings and all of your other assets work together to give you the whole fiscal picture.

This side of the balance sheet for most people remains fixed and is relatively easy to do, when they put their minds to it.

- Always remember that this process and document known as a family budget is only going to be as good as the data and updates you provide! When acquiring new assets, ensure that this side of the balance sheet is strengthened appropriately!

- Adjust your focus slightly to more in-depth and longer term. We live so much in the moment, especially if we purchase things or spend our money. We just look at the cost today and do not think of interest over time and this being the total cost of course.

- Actually, setting financial goals will also energize you, give you a reason to work towards something meaningful. You might even start to enjoy uncovering opportunities for frugal choices, 'penny-pinching' and what we prefer to call creative savings techniques!

- Become financially literate and master the family budget process, tools and worksheets, spending logs. Demystify some of the complexities and just try some fiscal responsibilities, without being overwhelmed by the intricacies of calculations and more.

Remember, there is always professional help out there, once you have gotten started, completed the grunt and groundwork to move in and on to a comprehensive consultation with a personal, professional financial planner, who can explain the lay of the land, impact of your situation and plan in more detail.

Most of them will offer the first consultation free to assess your situation for you. Most of them utilize state-of-the-art software and technology industry-related and customized tools that shed light on even the darkest situation, to find a little ray of hope and a couple of dollar at the end of the tunnel. There is a way out of the abyss.

- Family budgeting can be used to teach you good fiscal habits: get in the habit of paying in cash, using your credit cards only for emergencies.

Learn how to stop buying on impulse and use your willpower to walk away, say no thank you and leave it at that. Shop at wholesale and discount department stores. Respect your budget limits and stick to it. Buy generic medicine and support your discount pharmacy.

Always try to find ways to supplement your income, part-time jobs, your own business or rent room or floor in your house, offer storage, invest in real estate and take in a boarder or tenant.

Turn your thermostat way down in your house and turn off a few lights. Winterize your house from top to bottom. Eliminate and treat areas where heat and energy is lost. Cut back on home and cell phone use. Check insurance policies shop around and raise your deductible to lower your monthly bill.

In isolation, these probably do not have a lot of impact individually, but when they are combining in a well-planned, cleverly executed family budget, with discipline and consistency, they will start to make a difference and you will start to see the benefits and impact on your bottom line.

> • A family budget is a learning tool and process to empower individuals and families to better self-manage their financial resources, spending, cost cutting and household finances. In general you will be able to set-up your own personal or family budget. By tackling the skill and mastery of smart budgeting, you will have a greater understanding eventually of exactly where and by how much you need to adjust expenses to either live within your means, or know how much extra you need to maintain your current lifestyle.

> • Other family budgeting process steps will require you to be able to identify and categorize all your expenses and, coupled with an easy set-up and follow filling system, create the backdrop and framework for all future budgeting and fiscal planning at home or elsewhere.

> • Family budgeting is not something that is taught by parents or schools; however, it is such a simplistic concept, process and task that

it is almost unthinkable that we are not placing greater focus on it these days.

In the end, it's all about what you DO to make ends meet, which implies action. To be in charge of your finances; family budgeting gives you a sense of real understanding and control over your money, not the other way around. Money is a 'tool' and life necessity but it does not prescribe how you should live or spend it.

- Family budgets allow you to gain knowledge you would otherwise not have had at your fingertips, concerning your own and family finances. For example: Knowing where and what expenses you can affect or effectively change, to cut costs appropriately, timely and immediately in certain cases is very helpful.

- To enable your family budgeting process set up an easy and orderly log, record-keeping and filing system; and make spending notes often to track your money and habits. Trust me, we do not know where all our money goes. We are just certain of one thing and that it slips through out fingers, hands and pockets, cards and plastic, fast!

- Understanding, explaining and sharing the benefits of good budgeting with others is pivotal, to get them on-board and participating actively in the family budgeting process. Ask for their ideas and input. Two heads are better than one in most cases. They might think of savings opportunity, consolidations and or things to do without, that you did not even think about or considered for a second!

Here are some more family budgeting summary steps to remember:

- Identify and categorize all expenses – look at categories and line items, types and timing of expenses, amounts and budget accordingly. Remember categories like miscellaneous, discretionary, maintenance, emergency and others. These will also provide you with a little more flexibility when you do have to massage your money, budget and cash flow processes to meet need, demands and change.

It is of utmost importance that we are able as family budgeters to allocate and adjust expense items, prioritize need with foresight, discretion, informed choice and empowered confidence, stemming from core and in-depth knowledge and accurate information.

- Practice utilizing a basic budgeting framework and recording method in your family budgeting and formulate your very own personal and or simple 'Home Budget' or rough first draft of your financial situation – a kind of YOU ARE HERE situational analysis. Chances are you will see and learn something you did not know before.

- Distinguish between fixed, variable and discretional expenditure(s)

- Identify and categorize all expenses, breaking them into categories and line items, time-frames, other detailed sub-classifications and clustering.

- How to set-up housekeeping budgets and what to consider.

Identify hidden expenses.

- Identify areas of discretionary spending, habits and perhaps over-spending risk areas

- Setting up expenditure recording system that works for you

- Decide on the best way suitable for you and your family to monitor what you spend

- Set-up a very basic Home/Personal Budget Filing System

- Any calculations, formulas and budget principles you think will help you maximize and your cash flow and money-management

Another great way to learn about family budgeting is to ask around and to learn from others.

With the internet at our disposal, there are numerous reliable sources of practical, tried, tested and true tips, strategies and techniques to follow. We selected but a few to provide a sample.

Never underestimate the power of a shared experience!

Sometimes exploring a financial activity like family budgeting conceptually is not enough.

Getting a practical perspective, with some hands-on tips can be more meaningful that a close description or analysis.

There are lots of definitions, opinions and numerous books have been written on the subject of budgeting for families, by families and others. In our information-age, knowledge is power these days and lots of parents and professionals share and voice their opinions openly on the internet, sharing and growing the body of knowledge.

Here are Eleven Practical Suggestions and Tips:

1) Keep a record book as well as your bankbook

This can be done electronically or on paper, whatever works for you. It takes time and requires a lot of self-discipline. Start each month with the balance and enter every payment, etc. in advance, in the form of a calendar. It works well for most people due to the fact that they always have their actual working balance handy. Remember the comment about having your financial information at your fingertips? Here is a sure-fire way to get you on that path quickly.

2) Calendar Calculations

Putting regular bills on a calendar based on due dates and when salaries are received proves helpful. This helps specifically to get everything paid on time and keep in perspective where the money actually goes, since all miscellaneous expenses are also recorded.

3) Getting bills paid

Working out all the major and large bills (i.e., rent, car payment, insurance, etc.), dividing it up to every week, that amount is removed from the family 'paycheck'. Therefore, at the end of the month, there is need or risk to lose an entire paycheck to rent or car registration.

4) 1-2-3-4 Plan

Divide all bills weekly. A set amount goes to a savings account each week. When there is a 5th Friday in a month, you have a "free paycheck" to save.

5) Open a household account

In a second checking account, deposit a sum that covers your monthly expenses. Have all of your bills automatically withdrawn. This account acts as a holding cell for household obligations - the primary account is for day-to-day operations. Works for most! Be aware on this one that many banks have increased their bank fees in 2020. Don't do it if the bank charges you fees.

6) A timely budget

Get a notebook. List expenses and their due dates. Divide payments into small amounts & use labeled envelopes for payments and money storage. Reduce duplicate credit usage to 1 or 2 credit cards. Use the net for bill paying and to check your accounts.

7) Yearly savings

Making a list of all annual or once-a-year type bills (car registration, shots for pets, school pictures, etc.) and divide them by 12. Save this amount each month and, when one of these items come up, you have the money to pay it. No more surprises.

8) Save credit card receipts

Keep an envelope in the car for the credit cards you use. When you buy anything using a card, put the receipt in the envelope as soon as you enter the car. Keep changing the envelope every month. This will save you time and hassle when looking for receipts.

9) Only twice a month

Separate all bills to be paid on either the 1st or 15th of the month. This enables you to pay all bills at once and on time. An added bonus is that you will also immediately know how much money you have left over for entertainment, vacation and other discretionary items.

10) Split into Savings and Checking

Figure out a budget based on a savings account/ checking account split. Savings builds up for things like real estate taxes, vacations, and insurance. Checking is monthly (e.g. phone, groceries, etc.). Split your monthly income into the savings and checking accounts according to the budget. Savings amounts are strictly budgeted. The checking account is controlled by watching the balance until the next payday.

11) Respect your partners need for financial security

Everyone likes to buy their toys, but the overall financial security of the household needs to be considered first. I am not against toys; just save up the money first to buy them versus putting non-essential day-to-day expenses on credit.

An example of a toy in my relationship was the spouse's need to have a big expensive truck in the driveway. I was not against the truck, I was against the debt to purchase the truck when there was no money in the savings or money built up for college tuition. Be considerate of the overall family financial situation and provide financial security for your family.

Suggestions on family budgeting:

1) Stay busy after work

One "easy" way to avoid overspending and thus stay within your budget is to have something else to do after work. Get a second job that is fun, go to school, volunteer or get into great physical shape. The more you do, the less you will spend!

2) Watch those miscellaneous categories

Make sure you have enough well-defined categories to capture your true spending. Putting too much into a miscellaneous category makes it harder to track what you have spent and harder to control, especially the splurges!

3) Need

If you did not know you need it, you probably do not. Do not buy things just because they are on sale. If you had no use or want for it before you saw it on sale, then you will have no use for it later.

4) Save money for special occasions on a budget

Add up how much you will spend on Christmas, birthdays, etc. Treat that total like it was a debt and make payments to a savings account for special occasions. Be sure to select a specific day of the month that your payment is due and stick with an amount. Don't fall for peer pressure, it is OK to not make expensive gifts to everyone just because they do.

5) Don't Forget to Budget for Special Occasions

When forecasting your expenses, remember to include gift-giving occasions. Mother's Day, Valentine's Day, birthdays, Christmas, and anniversaries are good examples. If you plan to spend money on these occasions, remember to include this in your budget.

6) Don't use a debt to get out of another debt

Do not take out a consolidation loan to pay off your other debts. The point is to get out of it, not to squeeze them together and end up paying interest on the loan while paying off your debts. Try consulting a "free" debt counselor service first if you feel stuck.

7) Remember To Budget Time As Well

We have all heard "time is money." Well-spent time can be an investment. Take a few minutes to plan ways to save on bills - 15 or 20 min. researching lower rates on electricity or long distance can pay off. You will know when time spent is not worth it.

8) The envelope system

Total yearly/monthly bills, divide each into 12 months. Divide monthly amount into bi-weekly payments. Use envelope for each bill; put in cash every 2 weeks. Use only the cash in envelope till it is gone. Do not touch your account/debit card! Envelopes ONLY!

9) Good teeth cheaper

You can go to a dental school to have your teeth cleaned, filled, orthodontic work done, etc. The cost is approximately half what you would usually pay. Note: Make sure you have some extra time as this takes a little longer. You can do the same with hair dressers.

10) Avoid expensive friends

Avoid friends who want to go for drinks all the time or suggest an evening at home. The money you spend on drinks and snacks, can buy something better, or go into your savings account. Also avoid friends who want to have supper at your house because you are a "good cook" what that really means is that they are saving money while you are grocery shopping.

11) Keep Track of Your Expenses on a Daily Basis

Log in to your banking every single night before you go to bed. You can see what checks and/or debits from your debit card are posted and what the running balance is. Compare with what you have in your checkbook or with receipts. This only takes about 10 minutes.

Often people get into trouble when they try to keep a running total of what they have left in their head and get into trouble. This also assures you there are no fraudulent charges withdrawn from your account.

12) How To Live Within Your Budget

Organize, budget, and beat stress.

13) Know what you spend

Establishing a budget, and periodically entering all of your purchases into money managing software, should take the guesswork out of your finances. At the beginning, minor changes will most likely need to be made to your budget. Once you have a finalized budget, one person should be responsible for maintaining the budget and tracking finances. I sit down with my partner on a monthly basis and go over our financial results. If we are close to exceeding a budget line item during the month,

I will tell my partner and we adjust our spending accordingly.

14) Cut down on interest

With bills happening throughout the month, people can find themselves poor one part of the month, and rich during the other. My bank offers free online bill pay, so I take all of my bills, and divide it by 4. I then pay weekly, so I always have the same spending cash each paycheck. It also cuts down on the interest that accrues.

Sometimes, just listening to the opinions of others opens up our minds to other possibilities we have not thought of, read about or seen in any published material, Industry -related text-books or budget specialist tip sheets and 'how to' layouts. All the technical information, procedural and budgeting principles are extremely important if you want to ensure lasting and sustainable change. It is also undeniably true, that in this day and age, collaborating and connecting with others is how we learn.

Utilizing online sources, electronic publications and shared experiences, solving common problems together is definitely the wave of the future. Some providers online offer 'live' customer consultations.

Taking control of your finances should challenge, invigorate and excite you. You are taking charge of your life, getting your ducks in a row so to speak and traveling down the road of fiscal responsibility and re-connection.

It is mostly a money crunch or crisis situation that make us lean towards budgeting more. Handling a money crisis well and realizing that family budgeting is but one pieces of that puzzle, might be helpful. The expectations, problems faced, context and depth of the crisis, is as important as the steps, procedures, techniques, tools and budget worksheets you end up using.

Admitting that there is a problem is normally considered a good first step. Asking for help is a close second. Money-matters makes us do strange things. You are probably not the only one facing this situation. Therefore, take heart there is help out there. Even before getting to the how to steps for your own budget, work on your state of mind, immediate needs, concerns, dues and crisis. Consult a professional financial planner, who will assist you, in all likelihood, through and financial analysis of your situation, assembling facts and information, coming up with solutions, suggestions and alternatives you probably are not thinking of right now.

Even when not under pressure or in crisis, when setting up a family budget, gather your thought, emotions, data, receipts, statements, input from others, discuss, consult, assemble, synergize and prepare to succeed. Get the most appropriate, accurate information you possibly can before setting up any expense categories or filling out worksheets.

Get and extra set of eyes to look it over, you will not regret it.

Sober, even-keel, un-emotional, rational, clear-minded, level-headed and ready to take on any challenge – include setting up a personal and family budget, income, expense statements, asset-liability summaries, expense categories, line items, amounts, estimates and more. Committed to succeed, with a positive attitude and financial resourcefulness will serve you well in any situation, no matter what the money crunch or reason for your budgeting need may possibly be.

Take some risks when required. Be pro-active and explore your options. Do not hesitate to tackle controversial topics or expenditures, even if it can lead to conflict and disagreement. Couples and finances have always caused some difficulty, so it is all normal. Stabilize your situation, salvage what you can and move on, focus forward.

Family budgeting has the past, present, future continuum all covered.

I suggest eleven steps in any new money management endeavor you undertake where personal interest and stake is high:

> Step One: Change Your Expectations and be Realistic

> Step Two: Tell Yourself the Truth – Face the Music

Step Three: Decide How to Pay for Necessities – Stop-gap Solutions

Step Four: Identify Your Assets – all of them! They are there, we just need to go find them

Step Five: Discover How Much You Cost – this is how much you spend and your contribution to situation and circumstance

Step Six: Calculate What You Can Afford to Cost – cost cutting and balancing your budget

Step Seven: Call Your Creditors – negotiate your debt (go back and read the credit negotiating part in this book)

Step Eight: Paying Late Fees – pay bills on time to avoid late fees. If you can't pay the whole amount, pay a small portion and call the company and ask for waving the late fees. They do that if you show good faith

Step Nine: Create a Family Budget!

Step Ten: Do Not Ignore the Following: IRS, Parking tickets, Association Fees, Car payment, Immigration and other government affiliates that need to be pulled into your situation to assist you as best they can

Step Eleven: Manage Your Money Every Day

It is no surprise then, to even find the ever-popular 'budgeting' concepts among these listed must do's to re-collect, re-orient and return to fiscal freedom and avert further money- related crises!

How Should a Family Budget be Used

This question immediately suggests that it should be part of the whole family budgeting process. It is much part of the learning around setting it up, considering its usefulness, function and purpose.

Creating or setting up the budget is one thing. Sticking to it, effectively implementing, sustaining and if actual fact, in essence 'using' it is the ultimate goal and achievement. That is worth celebrating. Families have different ways again to use or refer to their family budgets.

For some it will be no more than a general guideline. For others it would constitute an absolute rule not to be bent or broken. Others still will use the family budget as a strategic planning tool to protect the interests of his/her family and plan for a full and happy life, setting a small amount aside for the future, invested smartly and securely, with confidence and pride.

The very day the family budget actually assists you in reducing your spending and making informed smart financial decisions that is the day you do not sit back and relax, but throw all your energy back in making it even better. This is an on-going, continuous improvement exercise, experiment and undertaking of your own making, design and creation!

It is very common to get discouraged when on the family budgeting path. The minute you feel you have taken strides forward, something will happen, a setback, unexpected upset or expense, breakdown, maintenance or replacement or car, appliance, major purchase or repair and many other setbacks will occur.

In a sense it makes families more robust, responsive and adaptable. Tracking your finances makes you aware of patterns and business cycles, cost and many other factors that affect hearth and home financial life and health. Rent increases, more expensive cigarettes or tax increases, higher gas or energy prices or increased mileage to and from work are but a few examples of these events and issues that might come up.

When faced with these challenges, problems or complexities, having your fingers on the pulse of your available resources, discretionary monies, savings, line of credit, rates, banking fees and more, will all help you make the right informed decision that is best for your family, at that time and act accordingly with diligence and confidence. You are in control of your financial situation and not the other way around. It enlightens and empowers you to do more with less!

Unpredictable pricing and fluctuating expense are not easy to reduce in any budget. Having this variation handy, spread over a period of time, can help you plan better and anticipate sudden spikes or higher expenditure during certain months of the year.

For example, the telephone bill is higher when the teenagers are home for the summer. Emergency, contingency and improvements are not priorities for most of us when we receive our paycheck.

To ensure a steady stream of into these categories make "saving for a rainy day" come to life and have some real impact and meaning in our financial planning.

Cutting non-essentials first is a good strategy. Alcohol, long distance phone calls, gifts, gardening and landscaping services, decorating costs, pet care needs, recreation and lottery tickets can all be good money-saving categories. The more line items you can include, in your cost reduction, the smaller the dollar-amount impact in each.

It should come as not surprise that by just cutting a little in each of these categories, families can easily save upwards of $240 per year without too much noticeable difference in their lifestyle or any major disruptions or sacrifices. If is less than1 % of your total spending, it should not really cause pain, grief or reason for worry.

Family budgets can also provide hints on how to save on non-essentials: Buying more or less of a product or service, comparison shopping for the lowers possible price, bulk and discount, sale, buying a lower-priced or no-name brand. Eliminating some gift giving (Christmas, birthdays, friends and family) is a way to save money.

Elimination of waste is another clever way to save money that is often overlooked, BUT not in the family budget. Thrown out food because too much was purchased or it spoils because at time of purchase it was not as fresh as it could have been. Spur-of-the-moment clothing purchases, too trendy, uncomfortable and not the right size perhaps?

Making an active effort to participate in the family budgeting process will carry its own rewards as well. Self-discipline and curbing your own spending will soon become second nature.

Anything from a small rent increase of a couple of dollars to an all-out job-loss can impact home life and finances, and not in a positive sense. The family budget offers you the opportunity to prepare somewhat for this, whether pro-active or responsive action follow. Flexibility and adaptability are bonuses with family budgeting.

It will spell out the reality, damage, impact, what needs to be done at the barest of minimums to get by and offer stop-gap solutions, practical and accessible, right away. It is not to say that it will have you not worrying about it! All of us will be concerned if this is our situation, but it will leave you more prepared to deals with the challenges head on and right away as opposed to wasting time wondering what to do and how bad it is.

A budget protects you against income reduction and inevitabilities.

In the case of job loss mentioned above there are also immediate realities to consider. Financial implications are huge for family life and the pressure is on. Family budgets and informed budgeted will tell you that this tool and time spent will be worth every penny if this were ever to happen to them.

Tackling normal spending categories first, reduced transportation costs, packing a lunch as opposed to having it in the cafeteria every day. Suspend all discretionary funding, move money in your accounts around to ensure liquid assets to cover basic expenses. Luxury items and recreation, sports and other leisure activities will be another category to find some budget dollars.

Maintenance and repair costs might be suspended or delayed, cost-cutting is never pleasant but the budgeting process makes it easier to know where the cushions and 'fat' is that can be trimmed or eaten away at, without risking heart and limb!

 Other positive job-changes like promotions and relocations could also have a lot of impact.

Taxes, relocation fees, buy-and-sell of homes, settling allowances, insurance, storage etc. they all add up. The family budget will help you assess your situation more clearly, leading to better decision-making and informed empowered choice.

Any discussion on 'How to set up a family budget', will be incomplete without a section dealing with debt and debt consolidation. Normally we use credit cards for a variety of good reasons, like convenience, business expenses, online commerce, instant accountability, unexpected bargains or expenses, medical and or other emergencies.

There are however, also very definite situations where plunging yourself deeper into debt is not a good idea at all: An expensive item you know you cannot afford (indulgence shopping). If you do not have the cash funds to purchase it, charging it is not going to make it easier for you to pay it! By putting it on plastic you just racked up the price and interest charges. Your budget will not thank you later for this one. Bad decisions often lead us down the wrong path.

You will be left facing paying for this choice for a couple of years down the road still.

Tele shopping or infomercials for gadgets and widgets is a bad decision.

When grocery shopping, pay cash rather than plastic, or you will most likely overspend.

Meals, drinks, nights out and other entertainment charges are all like the miscellaneous category in a budget. The balance and dues will just keep on piling up, if it is not tracked and monitored closely

If you are truly going to be budget-minded and money conscious while trying to get out of debt, consolidating or in debt-repair, avoid the plastic!

Check the interest rates on your card, consolidate accounts, go through the exercise of balance transfers et al. and follow the steps in the Credit portion of this book, on how best to approach credit of any sort while on the mend to financial freedom, reputation, repair and recovery.

For family budgeting purposes, credit cards are for EMERGENCIES ONLY and should not be used to pay for bills or luxury items. Carrying a high balance, missing a payment, paying less than the minimum or other faux pas, might negatively affect your credit rating and undermine all the other good work you were doing in your budgeting process.

Watch out for steeper late charges, higher rates, annual service fees, interest rates and charges, and cash advances.

Using your credit card at an ATM for a cash advance can sometimes not be convenient, as the rate and cash advance fees can total as much as 24% or higher. This is even more than loan sharks or other payday like loan providers.

Do not use credit cards for any of the following reasons: unbudgeted expenses you cannot pay for; having no cash savings to help you with unexpected expenses, consuming more than you can afford or impulse shopping.

Debt management and family budgeting actually fit like hand-in-glove together. They complement and strengthen each other if used appropriately and with caution, diligence and commitment to change.

It is advisable to get a handle very early on in your budgeting process on what exactly the debt situation is. For most people this is the most painful part of the process. Facing their monetary past and the aftermath of overspending, lack of budgeting and large debt!

Extreme care should be taken early on as well to protect your financial interest. Review your family budget spending categories and avoid debt by every means you can and not use it for living expenses.

A personal debt review can be painful, but is very necessary to assess the status quo or where you are now and how good or bad it is. What is the depth of your "obligation" category in your budget, where this will inevitably fall.

Debt is a wide concept, covering lots of things, including mortgage, car, credit cards and other retail credit card accounts and personal loans of any kind. IOU's from family or friends also have to be included, if you are honest about making a difference, repaying in a timely fashion and truly want to know how bad it really is!

Your summary sheet can carry the following headings: account, total amount due, monthly payment, total interest paid last year, and interest rate. Financial advisors call this a debt review register. It is painful to see this data, because it will clearly show the impact of bad financial decision-making. Interest paid gives you absolutely NO BENEFIT WHATSOEVER!

Strategies for debt and cash flow management in a family budget include:

• Consolidating all consumer debt (that is everything you owe, except for your mortgage) and making it a priority to pay it off in a timely fashion, getting reduced rates and maximizing your effort in wiping the financial slate clean.

• Paying off high-interest credit cards first, if you can. See if you can find a zero interest offer from a credit card company to transfer your high interest card. They usually offer a one or more years interest free. You can pay as much off as you can during that time and save a significant amount of money. If you can't do that, pay the smallest CC off first regardless of the interest charged. That way you have that out of the way.

• Use a line of credit if you can as the interest rates are typically lower

• Suspend any kind of spending on any credit card and establish good habits paying in cash for purchases

• Use all store-based cards wisely or not at all, if that is the disciplined approach you have chosen

- Store-based card often have no annual fees (they still have high interest rate and fees) and you could qualify for them even with a low credit score – showing restraint and good fiscal management by making your payments on time, every time and keeping the account up to date, will go a long way to regaining your confidence and repairing your credit.

- Utilize the service of a good credit counseling service to assist you and deal with your habitual over-spending and shopping addiction if necessary

- Use credit card statements for budgeting purposes for accuracy and tracking

- Loans are handled no differently – the strategy is pretty much the same: find the highest loan balance and the highest rate and start paying the latter first, if you can. If you can't do that, pay the smallest loan off first. This tactic will give you a much-needed mental boost.

- Avoid any new debt

- If after a six month period you have paid like clockwork, contact your creditors and negotiate a lower rate at that time to ease the burden a little bit

- Student and educational loans are approached as investments in your future and is a hybrid and shoulder debt category really. Loan-payback for all tuition debt needs to be included in your family budget. You can negotiate a student loan too, in fact, you can negotiate any loan. You just have to be perseverant in calling and asking for help. You'll be surprised of the results, especially if you talk nice and polite. Taking a second job, evenings and weekends might be an answer here. This might lead to better business opportunity later and higher paying jobs later in life!

Take heart. Family budgets are not here to depress you even further. The fact that you are taking pro-active measures to participate in your life, sends the right signals, not only to creditors and credit counselors, but also to the family members that care so deeply about you too!

Another popular topic for family budgets, is children and fun activities.

How to make the most of these togetherness opportunities, while living and functioning within limited means and on a budget, causes many money wise parents concern:

"The best things in life are FREE" – you just need to know where to find them, how to look and then enjoy them together. Being cash-strapped or budget-challenged should not minimize the FUN you as a family have together.

Prioritize it together with the other members and the children in the home (if they are older), discussing alternatives like picnics, walks, visiting a beach, lake or park close-by.

Look for locations with lots of open-area space, baseball fields, tennis courts, and basketball courts.

Use coupons for entertainment like movie rentals, miniature golf and other sports.

Coupons are given just about everywhere right now

Play board games with friends, arrange potlucks and play-dates.

Visit zoos and museums and outdoor summer concerts that are free of charge.

Add fun elements to choosing, like putting the activities in a hat and letting other choose what to do next.

Avoid window shopping, mall-crawling or expensive shops where you will be tempted to spend more money or leave feeling guilty that you cannot. One tactic I used when I wasn't able to afford anything was to go out shopping in a department store. I would spend many hrs. looking, trying on clothes and shoes without looking at the price, putting everything in the cart and, when I felt tired and done with it, instead of going to the cash register, I would take each one and ask myself if I can live without it. Each item received and Yes, meaning Yes, I can live without you! This tactic requires a lot of self control (and having zero money helps too). Today, I can afford to go buy pretty much what I need, yet, I am no longer wasteful.

For discounted, priced brand-name kids clothing, shopping at end of season sales is a real budgetary blessing!

Budget for one very special outing or event, you can do as a family and set aside a little extra if you can for that annual camping, local or road trip you plan for, in your family budgeting process each and every year.

Family budgets is not all doom and gloom. There are always ways to do little things together, make memories and invest time and attention in one another that costs absolutely nothing but time, a smile, a hug or two and a caring heart to share them all with!

Final Thoughts on Setting Up a Family Budget

None of us want to remain or be without money, short on cash, cash-strapped and not able to live well and or get the things we need, dream about and want. Family budgeting brings us one-step closer to our fiscal realities, while offering more than the direction and route, but also the tools and techniques to get to fiscal nirvana!

Most of us have an inherent want to protect what is rightfully ours. Our hard-earned cash is no exception here. We want to enable, as far as it is in our power, to utilize what little (or much) we do have to the best advantage and our family benefit overall. Family budgeting helps us do so with method, structure, elements and processes that enable success.

Family budgeting can assist have, and have nots alike make better financial decisions with a future perspective always in mind.

Building greater awareness of where our money actually goes, or ends up, can be enlightening and empowering at the same time. Some react with shock and horror, as they realize they are their own worst enemy. They bear witness to impulse-driven shopping and periods with no fiscal discipline.

Realizing that this course of action hurt you and your family in the long run, puts a sudden halt on the money flowing out typically! (even if the effect does not last too long!)

Although family budgeting can be overwhelming at first, the tools and techniques, process and steps to follow are fairly simple, straightforward and easy. Like so often said, it is not rocket science! We just need to have the right attitude, motivation and persistence to see and follow things through. Budget or bust!

Family budgeting can help you get, be and remain in control of your money and family's financial situation. Be kind to your pocketbook!

Family budgeting is not just about budgeting to the last cent and flying by the seat of your pants. It offers structure, wisdom, decision making and reward for the serious and tenacious amongst us. Taking it on as a major and regular task and priority will change your quality of life, sometimes without you even realizing it.

You are in it for the long haul! Take responsibility for spending. It this means laying down some groundrules in your household and cutting back on a couple of luxury items, that needs to be discussed, agreed upon and stuck to, to make your budget work and have an impact over time.

Family budgeting is one of those activities none of us really truly value, until we see or feel it makes a difference.

If you stick with it long enough, disciplined and committed, you WILL experience the dynamic impact and life altering influence of the process.

Trust the process! Trust yourself!

You will succeed like no other! You will always be proud of yourself in ways you never expected!

Tips and Ideas for Teaching Kids about Money

Studies show that even six month old kids can develop strategies that help them exert basic self-control and calm themselves down.

Emphasize some ideas early on to help your kids develop healthy money saving habits.

• Teach them to wait. Waiting is annoying for everyone but no one can escape it. When you're in a waiting situation, make them feel that's OK and normal, talk to them, make the time be fun. Getting all worked up and angry will make your kid do the same.

• Teaching your kids to wait is important when they want something "right now". Waiting is a crucial step in stopping impulse shopping later in life. Create a waiting game, like waiting for a chocolate bar for 15 minutes (have them look at the clock and do the wait).

• Have your kids save money in a safe place because is valuable. Emphasize the fact that money is valuable and needs to be cherished and protected.

• Have each member of the family have a personal saving "pot" and have a family "pot". Make it clear how important it is for each one to care for its own "pot". Set a regular date when each member of the family puts an amount in the family pot. Use the family money for pizza night and have the kids count the money needed to pay for the whole dinner. Have them handle the money to the cashier. Use paper bills and coins. Don't skip the coins even if they go out of circulation. Is very important for very young kids to learn the value of each coin.

• Teach your kids about trading. Trade something with them that's fair exchange in value, or have kids trade between themselves in fair value exchange. Don't do this without explanation of money value.

• If you have more than one kid, have them take turns and work for each other. One being the employer and the other being the employee. This can work out in just about everything they play with. Get them on that mindset.

• Organize a family fundraiser. By teaching your kids how to do a fundraiser, you teach them about money.

A bake sale, craft sale, car wash, garage sell, toy sale, anything you come up with. You can start by doing a small family event and go into neighborhood and later Gofund me.

• Do a family quiz game about money. Use allowance spending to create questions and when the right answers are given have a small reward, I emphasize small reward. Giving kids, especially very young kids big rewards teaches them to want more and more for relatively small effort.

Game idea: Q: Some things you need, some things you want. What items are in your room you need? What items are in your room you want?

Put $1 bill on the table. Ask the kids to come up with as many items as possible they have in their room that can be purchased with that one dollar. It's important for kids to actually own the object as opposed to think of it, they can relate better.

Put $10 bill on the table and do the same. You can continue with higher amounts depending on your kids age.

• Teach your kids the difference between buying one thing them the other. Say they want a bag of chips for $2, find something else that's interesting to them for the same amount and make them decide.

• Don't give in. This is very important. Kids can have a temper tantrum and manipulate you to get what they want.

• Give your little kids a loan when they want something big. That's right, a loan with interest. Have them negotiate a price with you and give them a loan. Make a pay back schedule and have them pay you back on that day each time.

- Once they learned the loan pay back game, go ahead and ask them for a loan. Is your turn to pay back on time each time with the interest negotiated. They will learn how it works both ways.

- Be careful with allowance. Many parents just commit to a certain amount to give to their kids just because everyone does it. Be very clear what the allowance is for and discuss how money gets spend. Every family is different and you have to decide why and what you'll give, but make it clear from the very beginning why are you giving the money. Always ask for entry on how they spend the allowance before you give them the next one. If you do this from the very beginning, you'll never have a problem later on and your child learns to budget just like that.

- Be consistent in everything you ask from the kids. If you promise to pay their allowance on the 10th, they will expect you to do so. There is not much paper cash used nowadays, everything seems to be online. Unfortunately, the best way to teach very young kids the value of money is still with real money as opposed to plastic.

- Insist that your kids clean their mess at all time. You might argue on this one, but, it works if you're consistent from the very beginning.

Money Saving Ideas

- Start with your food budget you created in previous chapters.

- Commit to spending a lot less shopping than you do now.

- Commit to grocery shopping like is a business.

- Make a day for grocery shopping and no matter what you're missing, don't go till that day.

- Never go grocery shopping without a list.

- Don't take your kids shopping, if possible, that way you can concentrate on your food business.

- Check your home for food before you go shopping. You might have stuff you forgot about.

- Don't just buy stuff because you feel like you deserve right now, or because it looks good. Stick with the list.

- Make a weekly menu and stick with it. When you have an appetite for something else, put it on a different week's menu.

- Already cut and packaged food is a lot more expensive and not that fresh anymore.

- Don't buy more than you need and let it go to waste.

- Don't ignore the food budget, it can throw your entire life budget out the window real fast.

- Don't ignore coupons. Use coupons everywhere you can. We live in a coupon world, use it to your advantage.

- If you find bulk items you usually consume on sale, buy and store but don't forget to use. Create your future menu wo to ith your bulk items in mind.

- If you can home grow some vegetables, do so but be prepared for a lot of work.

- If you have any relatives or friends who are growing vegetables, ask them for extras. You might be surprised how happy they are to share. You might ask for home canned goods too.

- Grocery stores have a discard for no longer fresh vegetable day, each week. Ask them if they can give you their extras. You will find a lot of still very good vegetables and the rest you can either compost or give to a gardener to compost in exchange for some fresh fruits or vegetables. You can incorporate your own leftovers for same reasons, this includes coffee and tea, but no meat and fat.

- You can go forage if you can find an area with fruit and berries along rural roads.

- Join a food co-op

- You can volunteer at a fruit/farm/ranch/ place in exchange for produce.

- Eggs seem to go up and down in prices and this year 2020 they went to a insane high price. When you find a good price, buy a few dozen extra and you can freeze them. The best way (I found by experimenting all and every way) is to freeze them after you whip them. That way, when they taw you won't get yellow frozen pieces. You can use them just like fresh for everything except when you only need whites or yellow. They scramble just like a fresh egg and taste the same.

- Make your own home/laundry/dishwasher cleaning powder. It can be a lot cheaper and with less chemicals. Check youtube for recipes.

- Always check your receipt or watch the scanner. There are a lot of mistakes.

- Track items you'd like to have in bulk and watch for sales.

- Chose the stores you shop wisely, don't just go because is convenient. Go for best price and quality after you calculate.

- Cook your food. If you don't know how to, learn. Start simple and you'll see how fast and easy it gets once you're organized. Cooking is easier than many people think. You just use the things you like to eat and combine them in every way you like to or feel. That's how cooking gets creative. Is really all in the spices. Use the spices you like and don't overthink. Use crock pot cooking for a while. Is easy, fun and so wonderful when you come home to a meal already done. You can put a frozen piece of meat, some vegetables and water in the pot when you leave for work in the morning and come home to a love affair.

• Be saving on paper towels, paper plates and napkins. They are going away real fast. Use washable kitchen towels, cloth napkins and real plates. If you have paper towels, be mindful and recycle the slightly used ones. You can rinse them and let them dry in a kitchen container for a second use.

• Slightly used plastic Ziploc bags can be washed and re-used. I wash them with soap and hot water and rinse well with a little vinegar water at the end.

• Track your restaurant habit.

• Sell things you no longer want or can live without. You can do garage sell or e-bay or other online markets.

• Sell other people's things. You can ask friends and neighbors if they have stuff they want to get rid of, sell for them and split profit. Many of them might be happy to get rid of and not even care to receive anything in return.

• What are your skills and hobbies? Can you use what you know to create extra income?

• Check your local area internet to find out what people might want in a service you can provide assistance with on par time basis.

• Check out money savings app, like www.Honey.com for coupons, www.savingstar.com for grocery store rebates

"Setting goals is the first step in turning the invisible into the visible"

- Tony Robbins

www.ingramcontent.com/pod-product-compliance
Lightning Source LLC
Chambersburg PA
CBHW071454040426
42444CB00008B/1332